STECK-VAUGHN

LEVEL

D

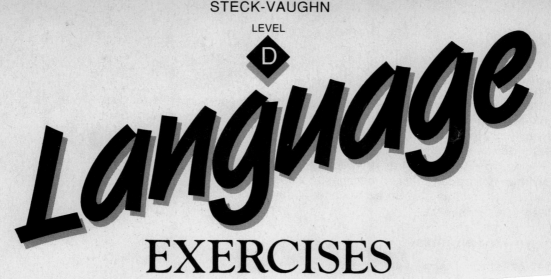

Language
EXERCISES

Betty Jones

Saranna Moeller

Cynthia T. Strauch

STECK-VAUGHN
COMPANY
A subsidiary of National Education Corporation

About the Authors

Saranna S. Moeller has been a teacher in the elementary grades for over twenty-five years. Moeller received her bachelor's degree in education from the University of Houston. She now operates the Refugio Learning Center in Texas.

Betty Jones earned her master's degree in education from Prairie View A & M University. Jones has been an elementary teacher for over twenty-five years.

Cynthia T. Strauch attained her master's degree in education at Texas A & I University. Strauch is also an experienced elementary school teacher, with over sixteen years of service.

Acknowledgments

Senior Editor: Diane Sharpe
Project Editor: Stephanie Muller
Product Development: The Wheetley Company, Inc.
Cover Design: Sue Heatly Design

Illustrations: Michael Krone
Photography: p. 18 Cindi Ellis; p. 35 Ricardo Chapa; p. 37 Cindi Ellis

Macmillan Publishing Company: Pronunciation Key, reprinted with permission of the publisher, from *Macmillan School Dictionary 1*. Copyright © 1990 Macmillan Publishing Company, a division of Macmillan, Inc.

LANGUAGE EXERCISES Series:

Level A/Pink	Level D/Gray	Level G/Gold
Level B/Orange	Level E/Red	Level H/Green
Level C/Violet	Level F/Blue	Review/Yellow

ISBN 0-8114-4193-8

7 8 9 PO 98 97 96 95 94 93

Table of Contents

UNIT 5 Composition

UNIT 6 Study Skills

Final Reviews

Synonyms

> ■ A **synonym** is a word that has the same or almost the same meaning as another word.
>   EXAMPLES: last—final; leave—go; prize—award

A. Rewrite these sentences. Use synonyms from the box below for the underlined words.

active	brave	common	glad
halt	large	stay	uncommon

1. The <u>ordinary</u> hive has many worker bees.

   _____

2. It is not <u>unusual</u> to find 80,000 <u>busy</u> workers in a colony.

   _____

3. The <u>fearless</u> worker bee will do anything to <u>stop</u> enemies of the hive.

   _____

4. The hive must <u>remain</u> warm, or the bees will die.

   _____

5. Farmers are <u>happy</u> to see <u>big</u> hives near their fields.

   _____

B. Find the pair of synonyms in each sentence. Write each pair on the lines.

1. My goal, or desire, is to study nature.

   _____   _____

2. I keep one journal on insects and another notebook on plants.

   _____   _____

3. I began building an ant colony on Monday and finished making it on Friday.

   _____   _____

4. I carry the entire, or whole, colony on the back of my bike.

   _____   _____

5. There is plenty of room for the tiny ants in the small box.

   _____   _____

Antonyms

> ■ An **antonym** is a word that has the opposite meaning of another word.   EXAMPLES: stop—go; yes—no; hot—cold

A. For each underlined word, circle the correct antonym at the end of the sentence.

1. The boys made a fast trip to town.   (quick   slow)
2. They had a funny story to tell their friends.   (sad   long)
3. Everyone who heard it was sure to laugh.   (chuckle   cry)
4. It's hard to believe they could do such a foolish thing.   (wise   funny)
5. They had only wanted clean uniforms for the game.   (dirty   bright)
6. They believed that looking good would help them win.   (play   lose)
7. They thought starch would brighten the colors.   (darken   highlight)
8. They were wrong.   (mistaken   right)
9. Now they couldn't stop laughing.   (end   start)
10. They had the only stiff uniforms in the league.   (solid   limp)

B. For each underlined word, write an antonym from the box.

1. dull knife   _____ knife
2. hard cheese   _____ cheese
3. correct answer   _____ answer
4. spend money   _____ money
5. remember homework   _____ homework
6. neat room   _____ room
7. finish chores   _____ chores
8. old clothes   _____ clothes
9. bottom line   _____ line
10. left side   _____ side
11. back door   _____ door
12. after lunch   _____ lunch

before
begin
forget
front
messy
new
right
save
sharp
soft
top
wrong

Homonyms

3

> ■ A **homonym** is a word that sounds like another word. However, it has a different meaning and is spelled differently.
> EXAMPLES: it's, its   their, there, and they're
> It's means "it is." **It's** a nice day.
> Its means "belonging to it." The dog hurt **its** leg.
>
> Their means "belonging to them." That is **their** house.
> There means "in or at that place." Put it **there**.
> They're means "they are." **They're** going to the game.

A. Write it's or its to complete each sentence.

1. The team starts _____ practice at noon.

2. The coach says _____ necessary to practice.

3. I don't think the players think _____ fun to practice.

4. Others say _____ exciting to watch the game from the sidelines.

5. The team is proud of _____ record.

6. If the team does _____ job, it will win.

7. I think _____ still a month until the championship game.

8. The team thinks _____ chance for winning the championship is good.

9. However, _____ too early to know for sure.

B. Write their, there, or they're to complete each sentence.

1. The girls rode _____ bikes home from school.

2. Now _____ getting ready to go camping.

3. Do you think _____ parents will drive them to camp?

4. Who put the suitcases _____ on the porch?

5. What time did _____ friends say they would meet them?

6. I hope _____ ready to camp out by the creek.

7. They think _____ ready for life in the woods.

8. I bet _____ parents aren't so sure.

More Homonyms

> ■ Remember that a **homonym** is a word that sounds like another
> word.   EXAMPLES: to, two, too   right, write   hear, here
> To means "toward" or "to do something." Go **to** the store.
> Two means "the number 2." Buy **two** gallons of milk.
> Too means "also" or "more than enough." It's **too** hot.
>
> Write means "to put words or numbers onto paper."
> Did you **write** the letter?
> Right means "correct" or "the opposite of left."
> Turn **right** at the corner.
>
> Hear means "listen." Didn't you **hear** me?
> Here means "in this place." Meet me **here** in one hour.

A. Write to, two, or too to complete each sentence.

1. The _____ cousins, Jeff and José, went _____ the
   skating rink.

2. There weren't _____ many people at the rink.

3. They walked inside and bought _____ tickets _____ skate.

4. "We need _____ rent skates, _____," said Jeff.

5. After they got their skates, they skated for _____ hours.

B. Write right or write to complete each sentence.

1. I'll _____ directions for finding my house.

2. You'll need a map to find the _____ roads.

3. Go ten miles and turn _____ at the bridge.

4. You're on the _____ road if you pass the shopping mall.

C. Write hear or here to complete each sentence.

1. "I can't _____ you because of the music," shouted Al.

2. "Come _____ so I can _____ you better," said Pete.

3. "Why did we come _____ to talk? I can't _____ anything,"
   said Al.

4. "Let's get out of _____," said Pete.

Multiple Meanings

5

> ■ Some words have more than one meaning. They are spelled the same, and often are pronounced the same, but they mean different things. The only way to know the meaning of these words is to see how they are used in a sentence.
> EXAMPLES: I **can** go.   Get the **can** of beans.

A. Circle the correct meaning for each underlined word.

1. She put the pad behind her back and leaned against it.
   pillow   walk softly

2. A tear rolled down her cheek.
   rip or pull apart   salty liquid from the eye

3. The rain continued to beat against the little cabin.
   strike over and over   to mix

4. As she listened, the warning bell began to ring.
   make the sound of a bell   narrow circle of metal worn on the finger

5. The pounding waves made a terrible racket.
   light bat used in sports   loud noise

6. Her cabin would soon be lost to the storm.
   attack   heavy winds with rain or snow

7. Her only hope was that someone would come and lead her to safety.
   soft metal   guide

B. Write a sentence for each meaning of the words given.

1. wind: blowing air

   _____

   wind: to tighten the spring of

   _____

2. rock: to move back and forth

   _____

   rock: a large stone

   _____

Prefixes

> ■ A **prefix** is a syllable added to the beginning of a word to change the meaning of the word.
>   EXAMPLES:
>   The prefix dis- means "not" or "the opposite of." **dis**appear
>   The prefix mis- means "bad(ly)" or "wrong(ly)." **mis**behave
>   The prefix re- means "again" or "back." **re**do
>   The prefix un- means "not" or "the opposite of." **un**friendly

A. Complete each sentence by adding un- or dis- to the word in parentheses.

1. Tabor the Great made a man _____ from the stage.   (appear)

2. The man looked _____ about what would happen to him.   (concerned)

3. He seemed _____ that he was even on the stage.   (aware)

4. The man vanished! The audience tried to _____ where he'd gone.   (cover)

5. But the man reappeared and was _____.   (harmed)

6. It would be hard to _____ an act as great as Tabor's.   (like)

7. No one could _____ with the fact that it had been a fine evening.   (agree)

B. Complete each sentence by adding mis- or re- to the word in parentheses.

1. I _____ the plan for the park at the edge of town.   (understood)

2. I didn't want to see a _____ of such fine land.   (use)

3. The plan is to _____ our town as it was long ago.   (create)

4. It will help us to _____ the history of the town.   (live)

5. I really _____ the plan.   (judged)

6. I should learn not to _____ before I know all the facts.   (act)

- A **suffix** is a syllable added to the end of a word to change the meaning of the word.
  EXAMPLES:
  The suffix -ful means "full of," "able to," or "the amount that will fill." hope**ful**, help**ful**, spoon**ful**

  The suffix -less means "without" or "not able to do." hope**less**, harm**less**

A. In each blank, write the word that matches the definition in parentheses.

| effortless | worthless | meaningful | endless |
| successful | careless | joyless | tireless |

1. Giving a _____ party is not always easy. (full of success)

2. When planning a party, I am _____. (not able to tire)

3. If the party is well planned, it looks _____. (without effort)

4. A _____ mistake can ruin a party. (without care)

5. A _____ game helps people to get into the spirit of the party.
   (full of meaning)

6. There is an _____ number of party games. (without end)

7. But all of the planning is _____ if no one comes.
   (without worth)

8. It would be a _____ evening if no one came to my party!
   (without joy)

B. Write a definition for the underlined word in each phrase.

1. colorless soap   _____ without color _____

2. bottomless pit   _____

3. sorrowful event   _____

4. beautiful car   _____

5. flavorless meal   _____

Compound Words 8

> ■ A **compound word** is a word formed by putting two or more words together.   EXAMPLES: railway, textbook

A. Write the two words that form each underlined compound word.

1. We are planning a picnic this <u>weekend</u>.

_____   _____

2. Aunt Tess is bringing her delicious <u>homemade</u> chicken.

_____   _____

3. My job is to bring the <u>watermelon</u>.

_____   _____

4. The picnic will be over at <u>sunset</u>.

_____   _____

B. Combine words from the box to form compound words.
Use the compound words to complete each sentence.

fire	front	watch	speaker	water	boat	place	tug	man	loud

1. The _____ inched slowly into the harbor.

2. The captain enjoyed looking at the buildings on the _____.

3. Using the _____, he called the crew to the deck.

4. As he waved to Mike, the night _____, he felt glad to be going home.

5. He would soon be home sitting in front of his warm _____.

C. Combine the words below to form four compound words. Use each word in a sentence of your own.

news	night	note	base	mid	ball	paper	book

1. _____   _____

2. _____   _____

3. _____   _____

4. _____   _____

Contractions

> ■ A **contraction** is a word formed by joining two other words. When the two words are joined, a letter or letters are left out. An **apostrophe** (') is used to show where the missing letter or letters would be.
>
>   EXAMPLE: I ~~would~~—I'd   he ~~is~~—he's   we ~~have~~—we've
>
> ■ The only contraction that breaks this rule is <u>won't</u>. <u>Won't</u> means "will not." The <u>i</u> becomes <u>o</u> when the <u>other</u> letters are dropped.

A. Rewrite each sentence using a contraction for the words in parentheses.

1. (I will) need volunteers for the school newspaper.

   _____

2. The first stories are due soon, so (we have) got to hurry.

   _____

3. (You will) each be given a section of the paper to work on.

   _____

4. The principal says (she is) looking forward to the first copy.

   _____

5. The English teacher says (he is) going to help us.

   _____

B. Underline the contraction in each sentence. Write the two words that make up each contraction.

1. Joe can't play in the basketball game tonight.

   _____   _____

2. He didn't remember to bring his uniform.

   _____   _____

3. The coach won't let him play without a uniform.

   _____   _____

4. Joe isn't happy about missing the game.

   _____   _____

5. No one thinks we'll win without Joe.

   _____   _____

A. Rewrite each sentence using a synonym for each underlined word.

1. The <u>large</u> dog gnawed on the <u>small</u> bone.

_____

2. He was not <u>frightened</u> by the <u>strange</u> sight.

_____

B. Rewrite each sentence using an antonym for each underlined word.

1. The <u>tiny</u> fire is <u>cold</u>. _____

2. The <u>old</u> joke made me <u>cry</u>. _____

C. Circle the correct word to complete each sentence.

1. I can (hear, here) the speaker very clearly.
2. I have (to, too, two) tickets (to, too, two) this event.
3. (Its, It's) interesting to see the statue on (its, it's) stand.
4. She asked us to (write, right) our names the (write, right) way.

D. Circle the correct meaning of each underlined word.

1. The <u>wind</u> howled through the valley.

    to coil or turn   moving air

2. He watched the river <u>wind</u> on its way.

    to coil or turn   moving air

E. Add <u>mis-</u>, <u>dis-</u>, <u>re-</u>, <u>un-</u>, <u>-ful</u>, or <u>-less</u> to the words in parentheses to complete each sentence.

1. I _____ (agree) with _____ (turning) books to the library late.

2. It is _____ (thought) to _____ (use) your right to the books.

3. Be _____ (thank) for _____ (limited) use of the library.

F. Write one sentence with a contraction and one with a compound word.

1. _____

2. _____

A. Rewrite the paragraph using synonyms for each underlined word.

The little man carried a large suitcase. He seemed to be trying to locate someone. Suddenly an auto screeched to a halt. The man grinned when he saw his best friend in the car.

_____

_____

_____

_____

B. Complete the paragraph. Write the correct homonym in each space.

I have no choice. I'll have to stay home until Mom gets

_____ (here, hear). Jeff is _____

(to, too, two) young _____ (to, too, two) be left

alone. _____ (There, They're, Their) is no one else

to watch him. _____ (Its, It's) wrong for you to think

I'd leave a child who's _____ (to, too, two) years

old alone. I'll wait to _____ (here, hear) from Mom.

Until then, _____ (there, they're, their) just going

to have to get along without me. I know this is the

_____ (write, right) thing to do.

C. Read the definitions of each word. Then write one sentence for each meaning given.

1. brush: tool for sweeping

_____

brush: bushes

_____

2. fly: insect

_____

fly: move through the air with wings

_____

D. Use mis-, dis-, un-, or -ful with one of the underlined words in each sentence to form a new word. Rewrite each sentence using the new word. Be sure the sentence keeps the same meaning.

1. I am <u>not happy</u> with the way the tape sounds.

   _____

2. I was <u>full of hope</u> that this tape would be good.

   _____

3. Now it seems that I <u>wrongly judged</u> it.

   _____

4. I'm still <u>not satisfied</u> with the way it sounds.

   _____

E. Combine the words below to form three compound words. Then use each word in a sentence of your own.

camp	post	light	fire	card	flash

1. _____

   _____

2. _____

   _____

3. _____

   _____

F. Underline all of the contractions in the paragraph. Then write each contraction and the two words from which it is made.

   I'm not going to take it any more! It's the third day in
   a row that I've had to do the dishes. You'd think I was an only
   child. We're just going to have to take turns.

1. _____   _____   _____
2. _____   _____   _____
3. _____   _____   _____
4. _____   _____   _____
5. _____   _____   _____

Recognizing a Sentence

■ A **sentence** is a group of words that expresses a complete thought.
    EXAMPLES: Ralph washed the car. He drove to the store.

A. Write <u>S</u> on the line if the group of words is a sentence.

_____ **1.** Sarah ran to the car.

_____ **2.** She was in a big hurry.

_____ **3.** All of a sudden.

_____ **4.** Sarah stared at the car.

_____ **5.** She couldn't believe her eyes.

_____ **6.** Three of the tires.

_____ **7.** Were completely flat.

_____ **8.** Sarah had no idea what caused the flats.

_____ **9.** Up the driveway toward the house.

_____ **10.** An open box of nails.

B. Write <u>S</u> on the line if the group of words is a sentence. If it is not a sentence, rewrite it as a sentence by adding whatever is needed.

1. The parents' club has its monthly meeting tonight.

_____

2. All of the parents.

_____

3. A slide show about fire drills will be shown.

_____

4. Following the slide show.

_____

5. The parents will take information home.

_____

Declarative and Interrogative Sentences

> - A sentence that makes a statement is called a **declarative sentence.**   EXAMPLE: We have two dogs.
> - A sentence that asks a question is called an **interrogative sentence.**   EXAMPLE: Do you have a dog?

A. Write underline{declarative} if the sentence makes a statement. Write underline{interrogative} if the sentence asks a question.

_____   **1.** How are you today?

_____   **2.** You didn't look well yesterday.

_____   **3.** I hope you're not getting sick.

_____   **4.** Are you getting enough rest?

_____   **5.** You really can't afford to get sick.

_____   **6.** Isn't the big game this week?

_____   **7.** You need to be healthy for this game.

_____   **8.** Will I see you in class?

_____   **9.** We are going to have a practice before the game.

_____   **10.** Are you ready for the game?

_____   **11.** Did you practice much?

_____   **12.** I practiced a lot.

_____   **13.** Do you think the practice will help?

_____   **14.** I get so nervous about big games.

_____   **15.** How do you stay so calm?

_____   **16.** Will you help me practice?

_____   **17.** Yes, I will.

_____   **18.** You're really a good friend.

B. Write one declarative sentence and one interrogative sentence about school.

1. _____

2. _____

Changing Sentences

> ■ A statement can be made into a question by changing the order of the words in the sentence. EXAMPLE: You are going to the show. Are you going to the show?
> ■ Sometimes a question word like <u>who</u>, <u>why</u>, <u>what</u>, <u>does</u>, or <u>how</u> must also be added to the statement to change it to a question. EXAMPLE: The show is two hours long. How long is the show?

A. Turn each statement into a question by changing the order of the words.

1. I am finished. _____

2. You shouldn't be finished. _____

3. This is taking too long. _____

4. You are leaving. _____

5. You can stay. _____

B. Turn the statements below into questions. You may change the order of the words and add question words as needed.

1. Joe starts his new job today.

   _____

2. He begins at nine o'clock.

   _____

3. He will leave home at eight o'clock.

   _____

4. Joe likes to work on cars.

   _____

5. Repairing cars is very interesting.

   _____

6. Joe is sure he will like this job.

   _____

7. Joe will do a good job.

   _____

Imperative and Exclamatory Sentences

- A sentence that gives a command is called an **imperative sentence.**
  EXAMPLES: Sit down. Read your book.
- A sentence that shows surprise or emotion is called an **exclamatory sentence.**
  EXAMPLES: Oh, you scared me! We won the game!

A. Write <u>imperative</u> if the sentence gives a command. Write <u>exclamatory</u> if the sentence shows surprise or emotion.

_____ 1. You go first, Jack.

_____ 2. Tell me if it's safe.

_____ 3. I'm scared!

_____ 4. Keep your voice down.

_____ 5. I can't see!

_____ 6. I'm lost!

_____ 7. Be quiet.

_____ 8. Come down here, Pete.

_____ 9. I'm falling!

_____ 10. Hurray, I'm out!

_____ 11. Close the window.

_____ 12. Watch out for that car.

B. Pretend that you are walking with a friend in a deep, dark forest. Write three imperative sentences and three exclamatory sentences.

1. _____

2. _____

3. _____

4. _____

5. _____

6. _____

Subjects and Predicates

■ Every sentence has two parts. The **subject** of a sentence tells who or what the sentence is about. The **predicate** tells what the subject does or what happens to the subject.
    EXAMPLE: The marching band won the state championship.
    Subject—The marching band; **Predicate**—won the state championship

A. Add a subject to each predicate to make a sentence.

1. _____ play tennis.

2. _____ run.

3. _____ returned the ball.

4. _____ won the game.

B. Add a predicate to each subject to make a sentence.

1. Players _____.

2. Some fans _____.

3. Coaches _____.

4. Judges _____.

C. Write subject or predicate to tell which part of each sentence is underlined.

_____ 1. Tennis is a game.

_____ 2. It is played with a racket.

_____ 3. The player swings the racket.

_____ 4. A ball is also needed.

_____ 5. Two or four players may play at one time.

_____ 6. Love means zero points in tennis.

_____ 7. A set is won in six games.

D. Draw one line under each subject and two lines under each predicate.

1. Tennis was invented by Major Walter Wingfield.

2. The game was called tennis-on-the-lawn.

3. Mary Outerbridge brought the game to the United States.

4. Tennis is a popular game.

5. Jimmy Connors is a famous tennis player.

6. You can play tennis, too.

Simple Subjects and Predicates

> - The **simple subject** is the main word in the subject part of a sentence. The simple subject is usually a noun or a pronoun.
> - The **simple predicate** is the main word or words in the predicate. The simple predicate is a verb and any helping verbs it may have.
>
> EXAMPLE: My cousin keeps his bike in the garage.
>
> **Simple Subject** — cousin
> **Simple Predicate** — keeps

A. Underline each subject. Then circle each simple subject within each subject.

1. The plans for a new car are made years ahead of time.
2. Many important decisions go into the design of a car.
3. Each part of the car is studied.
4. A clay model is made to show what the car will look like.

B. Underline each predicate. Then circle the simple predicate within each predicate.

1. Seven kinds of bears live in the world.
2. Most bears live in areas north of the equator.
3. Bears have little eyes.
4. Bears can live as long as thirty years.
5. A bear uses its claws to dig for food.
6. Brown bears usually eat grasses, berries, and nuts.
7. Seals and other animals are food for a polar bear.
8. Most bears sleep all winter.
9. Pandas are not really bears at all.

C. Write the simple subject and the simple predicate of each sentence.

1. The first basketball game was played in 1891.

   _____   _____

2. College teams played the sport in 1896.

   _____   _____

3. The first Olympic basketball game was in 1936.

   _____   _____

Simple and Compound Sentences

- A **simple sentence** has one subject and one predicate.
  EXAMPLE: Fresh paint brightens a room.
- A **compound sentence** is two simple sentences joined together by words such as and, but, so, and or.
  EXAMPLE: I painted the den, **and** Kim painted the kitchen.

A. Write simple or compound before each sentence.

_____ 1. We wanted to go camping, so we had to make plans.

_____ 2. Dad voted for Yosemite, but Sam voted for the Grand Canyon.

_____ 3. Sam got his way.

_____ 4. Finally, the day to start arrived.

_____ 5. Dad drove the camper, and Sam followed in the car.

_____ 6. The scenery was wonderful.

_____ 7. The canyon is almost too big to look real.

_____ 8. We wanted to camp at the rim, but it was too crowded.

_____ 9. We could sleep in the open, or we could use a tent.

_____ 10. We decided to use a tent.

B. Make a compound sentence by adding a simple sentence to each group of words below.

1. Sleeping outside is fun, but

   _____

2. The Grand Canyon is a great place to visit, and

   _____

3. We could hike down the canyon, or

   _____

4. Canyon burros are cute, but

   _____

> ■ Short sentences about the same subject can often be **combined** into one sentence. Connecting words such as and, but, and or may be used to combine sentences.
> EXAMPLE: Sam went to the store. Joan went to the store, too. They went in a red car. **Combined sentence**—Sam and Joan went to the store in a red car.

A. Combine each pair of sentences.

1. We have to write a report. The report is on history.

_____

2. My subject is the Civil War. My subject is Robert E. Lee.

_____

3. We must use the encyclopedia. We must use other books.

_____

4. I should stop wasting time. I should start my report.

_____

B. Combine each set of sentences into one sentence.

1. Juan bought a horse. It is big. The horse is brown.

_____

2. The horse is kept in a barn. The barn is red. The barn is old.

_____

3. Juan rides the horse. Lynn rides the horse. They ride in a field.

_____

C. Write three short sentences about an animal. Then combine your sentences into one sentence.

_____

_____

_____

_____

Avoiding Run-on Sentences

> - A **run-on sentence** is two or more sentences that run together without correct punctuation. Correct a run-on sentence by making separate sentences from its parts.
>   EXAMPLE: Many plants have seeds, the seeds grow into more plants, then those plants have seeds. **Correction**—Many plants have seeds. The seeds grow into more plants. Then those plants have seeds.

- **Rewrite each story by separating each run-on sentence.**

One morning we found a baby bird it had been knocked from its nest by high winds its mother was nowhere to be seen. It was too young to fly, we took it inside to care for it. We were excited about taking care of the bird, we didn't know what to do about feeding it.

1. _____
2. _____
3. _____
4. _____
5. _____
6. _____
7. _____

The bird's little mouth flew open so often that we could not find enough insects to feed it. Then Mom found that the little bird liked dog food it also liked little bits of cooked egg yolk we even made some nice worms out of hamburger meat.

1. _____
2. _____
3. _____
4. _____

**A. Write S on the line if the group of words is a sentence.
Write X̄ on the line if it is not a sentence.**

_____ **1.** The first railroad passenger cars.

_____ **2.** The B & O offered the first rail passenger service.

**B. Write interrogative if the sentence is a question. If the sentence is a
statement, rewrite it as a question.**

1. Joseph flew to Boston. _____

2. Have you ever been to Boston? _____

**C. Write imperative if the sentence is a command.
Write exclamatory if the sentence shows surprise or emotion.**

_____ **1.** I can't believe it!

_____ **2.** Be more careful in the future.

**D. Draw one line under the subject and two lines under the predicate of each
sentence. Then circle the simple subjects and the simple predicates.**

1. My cousin Lee plays hockey for the Hawks.

2. Lee practices early in the morning.

**E. Write simple if the sentence is a simple sentence. Write compound if the
sentence is a compound sentence.**

_____ **1.** Opal has a tricycle, and Ron has a wagon.

_____ **2.** They play with them all day.

F. Separate the run-on sentence into shorter sentences.

We played ball in the park we rode our bikes, then we
went home for dinner.

_____

_____

G. Combine the sentences into a single sentence.

Andrea likes chicken. She likes chicken that is baked.
Andrea likes rice with her chicken.

_____

_____

**A. Write sentence on the line if the group of words is a sentence.
If the group of words is not a sentence, rewrite it as a sentence.**

1. Lee and Kenji are from Japan. _____

2. Three years ago, they. _____

3. Now they. _____

4. Lee and Kenji like their new home. _____

B. Underline the declarative sentences. Write the interrogative sentences.

How much do you know about the flag? The stripes on
the flag stand for the first thirteen colonies. What do you
think the stars stand for? The stars represent the fifty states.
The colors have a meaning, too. White means freedom from
wrong. Red stands for courage. Blue stands for fairness.
Everything on the flag has a meaning. Did you know that?

1. _____

2. _____

3. _____

C. Rewrite the statements as questions.

1. Jetta ran to the grocery store.

_____

2. She bought bread and milk.

_____

3. She stopped at the park.

_____

4. Jetta was surprised at how long she was gone.

_____

**D. Write one imperative sentence and one exclamatory sentence
about an adventure.**

1. _____

2. _____

E. Draw one line under the subject and two lines under the predicate of each sentence. Then write the simple subject and the simple predicate of each sentence.

Fingerprints can prove who a person is. A light powder is used so fingerprints can be seen. Each person's fingerprints are different from anyone else's fingerprints. Even the fingerprints of twins are different. A person's fingerprints stay the same as he or she grows older.

1. _____   _____

2. _____   _____

3. _____   _____

4. _____   _____

5. _____   _____

F. Underline the compound sentences. Write the simple sentences.

The main product of Florida is citrus fruit. Citrus fruit needs warm weather to grow. Oranges are grown in Florida, and grapefruit are also grown there. Other fruits grow in Florida, but citrus fruit is still the main crop. Many vegetables are also grown in Florida.

1. _____

2. _____

3. _____

G. Rewrite the paragraph. Combine short sentences and separate run-on sentences.

Flies are interesting insects. The eyes of a fly have up to 400 parts they really see only motion and light. A fly has six legs. Each fly has six feet. Each foot has a pair of claws.

_____

_____

_____

_____

_____

_____

Nouns

> ■ A **noun** is a word that names a person, place, or thing.
>   EXAMPLES: person—girl, Anna; place—city, San Francisco;
>   thing—dog, Fido

A. Underline the two nouns in each sentence.

1. Mrs. Smith has a big job ahead.
2. She needs to plan the picnic for our school.
3. Mrs. Smith must find a big park.
4. The students always enjoy the picnic.
5. It is a big event every year.
6. Mr. Smith is planning some games.
7. He will set up a net for volleyball.
8. Margie will make the hamburgers.
9. Mrs. Smith finally picked Riverview Park.
10. The park is on the Mississippi River.

B. Tell what each underlined noun is by writing person, place, or thing.

_____ 1. Buttons the dog

_____ 2. my brother John

_____ 3. the neighbor's uncle

_____ 4. 472 Elm Street

_____ 5. Orville's friend

_____ 6. Morris the cat

_____ 7. the city of Trenton

_____ 8. presented by the mayor

_____ 9. Washington, D.C.

_____ 10. my friend's sister

_____ 11. the state of Utah

_____ 12. a large cloud

_____ 13. a happy clown

Proper and Common Nouns

> - A **proper noun** names a particular person, place, or thing. It begins with a capital letter.
>   EXAMPLES: person—Mary; place—Dayton; thing—Queenie
> - A **common noun** does not name a particular person, place, or thing.
>   EXAMPLES: person—girl; place—city; thing—dog

A. Underline the common nouns in each sentence.

1. Aunt Monica will visit for the holidays.
2. She loves Thanksgiving in the country.
3. My aunt is always a welcome visitor.
4. Her stories about New York are interesting.
5. This year, she is bringing Dr. Alvarado with her.

B. Underline the proper nouns in each sentence.

1. Dr. Alvarado is a doctor in New York.
2. She works at Parkside Hospital.
3. In September, she's going to teach a class in medicine.
4. The class will be at Roosevelt University in Queens, New York.
5. The students come from all over the United States.

C. Write a proper noun for each common noun given.

1. dog _____Spot_____
2. country _____
3. name _____
4. day _____
5. city _____
6. holiday _____
7. month _____
8. uncle _____
9. cat _____
10. friend _____
11. state _____
12. father _____
13. game _____
14. street _____
15. planet _____
16. school _____
17. teacher _____
18. continent _____
19. president _____
20. magazine _____

Singular and Plural Nouns

- A **singular noun** names one person, place, or thing.
- A **plural noun** names more than one person, place, or thing.
- Add -s to most nouns to make them plural.
  - EXAMPLE: dog—dogs
- Add -es to nouns ending in s, z, x, ch, or sh to make them plural.
  - EXAMPLES: dress—dresses, box—boxes
- If a noun ends in a vowel and y, add -s to make it plural. If the noun ends in a consonant and y, change the y to i and add -es.
  - EXAMPLES: bay—bays, party—parties
- If a noun ends with the f sound, change the f to v and add -es.
  - EXAMPLE: calf—calves
- Sometimes the entire spelling is changed to form a plural noun.
  - EXAMPLES: child—children, goose—geese, mouse—mice

A. Write S before each singular noun below. Then write its plural form. Write P before each plural noun. Then write its singular form. You may wish to check the spellings in a dictionary.

_____ 1. porch _____

_____ 2. chair _____

_____ 3. girls _____

_____ 4. wife _____

_____ 5. flies _____

_____ 6. sky _____

_____ 7. foxes _____

_____ 8. halves _____

_____ 9. pencil _____

_____ 10. alley _____

_____ 11. leaves _____

_____ 12. pouch _____

_____ 13. inches _____

_____ 14. shelf _____

B. Circle the correct noun in parentheses. Write singular or plural on the lines.

_____ 1. All of the (girl, girls) sat on the right side.

_____ 2. Joan's (desk, desks) was the second one.

_____ 3. There was only one (teacher, teachers).

_____ 4. Two (child, children) wrote on slate boards.

_____ 5. The class was held in one (room, rooms).

_____ 6. No one rode a (bus, buses) to school.

Singular Possessive Nouns

> - A **possessive noun** is a noun that tells who or what owns something.
> - Add an **apostrophe** (') and an -s to the end of most singular nouns to show that they are possessive nouns.
>   EXAMPLES: Tony's house, the dog's bone

A. Rewrite each of the phrases below using a possessive noun.

1. the house of my aunt   _____ my aunt's house _____

2. the dog my cousin has _____

3. the books belonging to my uncle _____

4. the bicycle of my grandmother _____

5. an apron belonging to the cook _____

B. Write the correct possessive form of the word in parentheses to complete each sentence.

1. (Jerry) _____ dog was lost.

2. The (dog) _____ leash had torn.

3. (Chad) _____ dad will look for him.

4. Maybe he is in the (neighbor) _____ yard.

5. Look, he's in the police (officer) _____ car!

C. Write the correct possessive noun to complete the second sentence in each pair of sentences.

1. The store is having a sale. The _____ sale will last a week.

2. Lisa bought a coat. _____ coat has a hood.

3. A clerk helped Lisa. The _____ job was to help people.

4. One shopping bag broke. The _____ contents spilled.

5. Another woman helped her. Lisa was grateful for the

   _____ kindness.

> - A **plural possessive** noun shows ownership by more than one person or thing.
> - If a plural noun does not end in -s, the possessive is formed by adding an apostrophe and an -s (**'s**) to the noun.
>   EXAMPLE: men's teams
> - If a plural noun ends in -s, the possessive is usually formed by simply adding an apostrophe after the -s (**s'**).
>   EXAMPLE: birds' nests

A. Write the correct plural possessive form of the word in parentheses to complete each sentence.

1. My (sisters) _____ band is very popular.

2. The (uniforms) _____ colors are beautiful.

3. The band plays for (parents) _____ clubs.

4. The (members) _____ cheering was loud.

5. The (instruments) _____ sounds were perfect.

B. Write the correct possessive noun to complete the second sentence in each pair of sentences.

1. Uncle Fred and Aunt Ida are farmers. _____Farmers'_____ work can be very hard.

2. The children help on the farm. Uncle Fred depends

   on the _____ help.

3. There are three ponds on the farm. The _____ water is very clear.

4. Uncle Fred keeps many sheep on his farm. He prepares the

   _____ food.

5. He gets milk from his cows. The _____ milking time is very early.

6. Three huge barns hold the animals. Painting the _____ walls is a hard job.

Action Verbs

> ■ The **verb** is the main word in the predicate. If the verb tells an action that the subject is doing, it is called an **action verb**.
> EXAMPLES: Children **play** in the park. The squirrel **ran** up the tree.

A. Underline the action verb in each sentence.

1. Rex jumped at Tiger.
2. Tiger leaped for the tree.
3. Rex snapped back at the end of his rope.
4. Tiger quickly spun around.
5. Tiger arched her back.
6. Rex pulled against his rope.
7. Tiger danced sideways.
8. Rex howled loudly.
9. Then Tiger licked a furry paw.
10. She yawned slowly.
11. Rex chewed at the old rope.
12. He snarled at the cat.
13. Tiger teased Rex even more.
14. Rex pulled against the rope again.
15. Suddenly, it snapped.
16. Tiger shot into the air.
17. Rex bounded across the yard.
18. Tiger scrambled up the tree just in time.

B. Complete each sentence by adding a predicate with an action verb to each subject.

1. The captain of the team _____.

2. The coach _____.

3. All of the team members _____.

4. The fans _____.

5. The scorekeeper _____.

6. Everyone _____.

Linking Verbs

■ A **linking verb** does not show action. Instead, it links the subject to a word that either describes the subject or gives the subject another name. If a verb can be replaced by one of the verbs of being (<u>am</u>, <u>is</u>, <u>are</u>, <u>was</u>, <u>were</u>), then it is a linking verb.

EXAMPLES: Football **is** exciting. (<u>Exciting</u> describes football.)
They **were** a tired group. (<u>Group</u> is another name for <u>They</u>.)
Yoko **grew** tired. (<u>Grew</u> can be replaced by <u>is</u> without changing the sentence.)

A. Complete each sentence with a different linking verb from the box.

are	feel	is	seem	sound
become	grow	look	smells	taste

1. Spring _____ a wonderful time of year.

2. The days _____ warm.

3. The air _____ fresh.

4. The flowers _____ pretty.

5. The evenings _____ lighter.

6. Spring vegetables _____ fresh.

7. The birds _____ cheerful.

8. We _____ more active.

B. Write <u>L</u> in front of each sentence that has a linking verb.

_____ 1. Marty is a club member.

_____ 2. He is left-handed.

_____ 3. All of the club members are left-handed.

_____ 4. They each write with their left hand.

_____ 5. They are a busy group.

_____ 6. The members meet on Fridays.

> ■ A **helping verb** is sometimes used to help the main verb of a sentence. Helping verbs are often forms of the verb to be—am, is, are, was, were. The verbs has, have, and had are also used as helping verbs.　　EXAMPLES: Jerry **has** gone to the store. I **am** watching for the bus.

■ **Circle the helping verb and underline the main verb in each sentence.**

1. For a long time, we had wanted to give Sherry a surprise party.

2. We had planned the party in the park the day before her birthday.

3. She has gone to the park almost every day.

4. We were waiting for her there.

5. Sherry was raking her neighbor's yard.

6. We were looking around the park for her.

7. We couldn't find her.

8. We were forced to make other plans.

9. So Sherry was given her surprise party on her birthday.

10. Juana is going to the zoo today.

11. She has gone there once before.

12. Jack had told her to see the monkeys.

13. She was going last week.

14. She had planned a picnic.

15. I am going to the zoo with her.

16. I have seen the zoo before.

17. We are taking the bus.

18. Jack is meeting us there.

19. He is riding his bike.

20. We are looking forward to the zoo!

Verb Tenses

> - The **tense** of a verb tells the time expressed by the verb.
>   There are three tenses—present, past, and future.
> - **Present tense** tells about what is happening now.
>   EXAMPLE: I **am walking** my dog. I **walk** my dog.
> - **Past tense** tells about something that happened before.
>   EXAMPLE: I **walked** my dog yesterday.
> - **Future tense** tells about something that will happen.
>   EXAMPLE: I **will walk** my dog tonight.

A. Write present, past, or future to tell the tense of each underlined verb.

_____ 1. Jules Verne <u>wrote</u> about going to the moon.

_____ 2. Space ships <u>were</u> still in the future.

_____ 3. Now we <u>can fly</u> to the moon.

_____ 4. A space shuttle <u>will leave</u> tomorrow.

_____ 5. It <u>is stationed</u> in Florida.

_____ 6. The shuttle <u>helped</u> us explore space.

_____ 7. It <u>will help</u> us settle in space.

_____ 8. The shuttle <u>is taking</u> off now.

_____ 9. It <u>will return</u> in a week.

_____ 10. I <u>will go</u> to watch it land.

_____ 11. It <u>will be</u> a sight to remember.

B. Complete each sentence by writing a verb in the tense shown in parentheses.

(past)   1. Joy _____ in the garden.

(present) 2. She _____ gardening.

(future)   3. The garden _____ many vegetables.

(present) 4. Joy _____ the garden to be nice.

(future)   5. She _____ flowers next week.

(past)   6. She _____ the garden last week.

> - The past tense of a **regular verb** is usually formed by adding -ed.
>   EXAMPLE: jump—jumped
> - If the word ends with a single consonant that has one vowel before it, double the final consonant and add -ed.
>   EXAMPLE: skip—skipped
> - If the word ends with a silent e, drop the e and add -ed.
>   EXAMPLE: bake—baked
> - If the root word ends in y, change the y to i and add -ed.
>   EXAMPLE: worry—worried

A. Write the past tense of each verb to complete each sentence.

1. Ms. Willis (look) _____ out the window.

2. She (gasp) _____ at what she saw.

3. A hot-air balloon (settle) _____ onto her lawn.

4. Two men (step) _____ from the balloon.

5. Ms. Willis (hurry) _____ across the yard.

6. The balloon's basket (crush) _____ her flower bed.

7. One man (scratch) _____ his head in wonder.

8. He said they were (head) _____ for the fairgrounds.

9. The wind had (change) _____ .

10. "We (drop) _____ in here instead," he said.

B. Rewrite each phrase in the past tense.

1. sail the boat

_____

2. steer a straight course

_____

3. carry the sail

_____

4. enjoy the fresh air and sunshine

_____

Irregular Verbs

> ■ Do not add -ed to form the past tense of **irregular verbs.**
> Change the spelling in a different way.   EXAMPLES:

Present	Past	Present	Past	Present	Past
begin	began	give	gave	say	said
break	broke	go	went	see	saw
choose	chose	grow	grew	sit	sat
come	came	know	knew	take	took
fall	fell	leave	left	throw	threw
fly	flew	run	ran	write	wrote

■ **Complete each sentence by writing the past tense of the verb in parentheses.**

1. I'm surprised coach (choose) _____ me for the team.

2. The season (begin) _____ badly.

3. The coach (come) _____ to see me play.

4. I (throw) _____ a wild ball.

5. Then I (grow) _____ more nervous.

6. At bat, I (take) _____ a wild swing.

7. I never even (see) _____ the ball.

8. By that time, I almost (give) _____ up.

9. The coach just (sit) _____ and watched.

10. I thought I (know) _____ what he was thinking.

11. One ball (fly) _____ right over my head.

12. Then I (break) _____ the bat.

13. I finally hit one that (go) _____ out of the park.

14. I got so excited, I (run) _____ the bases backwards.

15. My face (fall) _____ when I realized what I had done.

16. Coach (say) _____ I should talk to him later.

17. I couldn't believe it when he (write) _____ my name on the list!

18. I was very proud when I (leave) _____ the park that day.

> - The **subject** and **verb** of a sentence must agree in number.
> - A **singular** subject must have a singular verb.
> - A **plural** subject must have a plural verb.
> - You and I must have a plural verb.
>   EXAMPLES: Mike **hits**. They **hit**. I **hit**. You **hit**.
> - The singular form of a verb usually ends in -s or -es. Add -es to verbs that end in -s, -x, -z, -sh, and -ch.
>   EXAMPLES: Juan **watches** the game. Amy **waxes** the car.

- **Circle the verb that agrees with the subject of each sentence. Write singular or plural to show the number of the subject and verb.**

  1. Chickens (eat, eats) grain. _____plural_____

  2. A chicken (lives, live) on the ground. _____

  3. They (flies, fly) very little. _____

  4. A farmer (feeds, feed) the chickens every day. _____

  5. Chickens (scratches, scratch) the ground for food. _____

  6. Forest fires (causes, cause) damage every year. _____

  7. A forest fire (destroys, destroy) large areas. _____

  8. People (fights, fight) a fire with water and chemicals. _____

  9. A firebreak (slows, slow) down a fire. _____

  10. A river (acts, act) as a firebreak. _____

  11. Airplanes (drops, drop) water on forest fires. _____

  12. A firefighter always (watches, watch) for danger. _____

  13. High winds (spreads, spread) forest fires. _____

  14. A forest fire (kills, kill) many trees. _____

  15. Many animals (loses, lose) their homes. _____

  16. A forest (need, needs) many seasons to recover. _____

  17. Responsible people (helps, help) prevent forest fires. _____

Making Subjects and Linking Verbs Agree

- A **linking verb** is either singular or plural. The linking verb must match the subject of the sentence in number.
  EXAMPLES: Singular—Mario **is** in fourth grade. Plural—The twins **are** in fourth grade.
- A linking verb can be in the present tense or past tense.
  EXAMPLES: Present tense—Mario **is** in fourth grade.
  Past tense—Mario **was** in third grade last year.
- Use there is or there was with one person, place, or thing.
- Use there are or there were with more than one.
  EXAMPLES: There **is** a movie tonight. There **are** many kinds of birds.

A. Write am, is, are, was, or were to complete each sentence.

1. My cat _____was_____ in the garden one day.

2. I _____ sure I saw her wiggle her whiskers.

3. Her whiskers _____ shorter when she was a kitten.

4. A whisker _____ an organ of touch.

5. Whiskers _____ important to a cat.

6. My cat's whiskers _____ very long.

7. Her fur _____ very long, too.

8. I think my cat _____ beautiful!

B. Write There is, There are, There was, or There were to complete each sentence.

1. _____ many kinds of horses.

2. _____ no horses in America at one time.

3. _____ a horse called the pinto that is spotted.

4. _____ an Indian tribe long ago that raised pintos.

5. _____ pinto horse clubs that you can join today.

6. _____ a pinto club meeting every year.

7. _____ people working to save the pinto horse.

8. _____ other horse clubs to join, too.

Subject Pronouns

> - A **pronoun** is a word that takes the place of a noun.
> - A **subject pronoun** is used as the subject of a sentence or as part of the subject of a sentence. The subject pronouns are I, you, he, she, it, we, and they.
>   EXAMPLES: **We** went to class. Shelly and **I** did homework together. **He** is going to help us.

A. Underline the subject pronoun in each sentence.

1. She rode her bike to school almost every day.
2. It was a beautiful ten-speed.
3. They go as fast as the wind.
4. You can go anywhere on a bike like that.
5. We wanted to ride the bike.
6. I asked for a ride.
7. He got to ride first.
8. Then I got to ride.

B. Complete each sentence by writing a subject pronoun to replace the word or words in parentheses. Pretend you are Bill.

1. Jeff and (Bill) _____I_____ left early for school.

2. (Jeff and I) _____ had a test to study for.

3. (Jeff) _____ had studied, but I hadn't.

4. (The test) _____ was on plants.

5. (Plants) _____ are important to study.

6. "Which part are (Bill) _____ studying?" Jeff asked.

7. (Mrs. Hobart) _____ says this is an important test.

8. (Bill) _____ am going to study hard.

C. Write three sentences of your own using subject pronouns.

1. _____

2. _____

3. _____

> ▪ An **object pronoun** is used after an action verb or after words such as <u>to</u>, <u>with</u>, <u>for</u>, and <u>by</u>. The object pronouns are <u>me</u>, <u>you</u>, <u>him</u>, <u>her</u>, <u>it</u>, <u>us</u>, and <u>them</u>.   EXAMPLES: Jim told **him** to start. Alex bought the present for **her**.

A. Underline the object pronoun in each sentence.

1. Jeff won it in record time.
2. The speed of the run surprised us.
3. Jeff beat me by a mile.
4. Maria caught us in the last lap.
5. The coach will give them the prize.
6. The speech will be made by you.
7. Then a special prize will be given to him.
8. Coach told me the prize is a blue ribbon.

B. Complete each sentence by writing an object pronoun to replace the word or words in parentheses.

1. The teacher told (I) _____ to read my report.
2. I told (Mr. Sheen) _____ that the report wasn't ready.
3. Mr. Sheen asked when (the report) _____ would be finished.
4. He had warned (our class) _____ that the reports were due.
5. Some of (the reports) _____ were done.
6. A few students offered to read (their reports) _____.
7. The class listened to (Sonja) _____.
8. Mr. Sheen said he wanted (the reports) _____ all finished by Friday.

C. Write four sentences of your own using object pronouns.

1. _____
2. _____
3. _____
4. _____

> ■ Remember that a pronoun is a word that takes the place of a noun.
> ■ A subject pronoun is used as the subject of a sentence.
> ■ An object pronoun is used after an action verb, or after words such as <u>to</u>, <u>with</u>, <u>for</u>, and <u>by</u>.
>   EXAMPLE: **Sam** gave **the gift** to **the boys. He** gave **it** to **them.**

■ **Choose the correct pronoun to replace the underlined nouns in each sentence. Then rewrite each sentence, using the pronoun. You may use a pronoun more than once.**

| He | We | She | It | him | her | they | them | us |

1. <u>Mrs. Beck</u> arranged for a trip to the science museum.

   _____

2. <u>The bus</u> would have room for the whole class.

   _____

3. All of the plans would be made by <u>Mrs. Beck</u>.

   _____

4. <u>Phil</u> wanted to see the aquarium.

   _____

5. Then <u>Ellen and John</u> wanted to see the dinosaur bones.

   _____

6. Mrs. Beck asked if <u>the students</u> wanted to take lunches.

   _____

7. Everyone wanted to take lunches except <u>Craig and Pia</u>.

   _____

8. The teacher asked <u>Jim and me</u> to bring a notebook.

   _____

9. Jim and I gave the notebook to <u>the bus driver</u>.

   _____

10. <u>My friends and I</u> couldn't wait to go on the trip.

   _____

Possessive Pronouns

35

> ■ A **possessive pronoun** is used to show who or what owns something. The possessive pronouns are <u>my</u>, <u>our</u>, <u>your</u>, <u>his</u>, <u>her</u>, <u>its</u>, and <u>their</u>.
>
> EXAMPLES: Is this **your** coat? **His** cold is getting better.

■ **Complete each sentence by writing the correct possessive pronoun.**

1. _____ family and I were going camping.

2. Suddenly _____ car stalled in a dark forest.

3. _____ engine just would not run.

4. _____ family was stuck.

5. Dad almost lost _____ temper.

6. He didn't expect this from _____ car.

7. Mom spoke, and _____ voice made everyone quiet.

8. We held _____ tongues.

9. "_____ hands are trembling," Dad said to Mom.

10. "So are _____ hands," Mom answered.

11. "Look at the bears with _____ paws up in the air," said Mom.

12. Dad tried to start _____ car.

13. Mom held _____ breath while the bears looked at us.

14. The mother bear turned _____ cubs toward the woods.

15. _____ growls could be heard through the car windows.

16. We hid _____ heads below the windows.

17. One cub turned _____ head toward us.

18. I tried to get _____ camera out, but I couldn't.

19. _____ strap was caught on something.

20. "You can tell _____ class about your adventure when we

get back," said Dad.

Adjectives

36

> ■ An **adjective** is a word that describes a noun. Adjectives tell **which one, what kind,** or **how many.**
> EXAMPLES: **happy** person, **brown** dog, **four** cars

A. Circle the two adjectives in each sentence.

1. The big tiger chased the tiny mouse.
2. His sharp teeth flashed in the bright light.
3. The scared mouse ran through the small hole.
4. The speeding tiger slipped on the wet floor.
5. The tired mouse hid in a dark corner.
6. The damp tiger left in a big hurry.
7. The little mouse had a wide smile.

B. Add an adjective to each sentence in these paragraphs.

beautiful	green	Many	sparkling
fierce	dark	Gentle	Wild

_____ people go to the _____

national parks. They see _____ streams and

_____ forests. _____ animals roam

freely on _____ meadows. _____

deer and _____ bears both live in the forests.

bare	red	shaky	soft	thick
best	wooden	six	strong	young

The _____ boy climbed the _____ ladder. A

_____ wind blew the _____ branches. His

_____ friend steadied the _____ ladder. He picked

_____ _____ apples. The _____ leaves

tickled his _____ arm.

Adjectives That Compare

- Sometimes adjectives are used to compare one thing to another.
- Most adjectives that compare two things end in -er.
  EXAMPLE: The red chair is **bigger** than the blue chair.
- Most adjectives that compare more than two things end in -est.
  EXAMPLE: That chair is the **biggest** chair in the store.

A. Circle the correct adjective in each sentence.

1. Jean's puppy is the (smaller, smallest) of all the puppies.
2. He is (smaller, smallest) than his brother.
3. Toby was the (cuter, cutest) name Jean could think of.
4. Toby looked (funnier, funniest) than his sister.
5. He had the (whiter, whitest) fur of all the puppies.
6. Toby had the (longer, longest) ears Jean had ever seen.
7. Jean soon learned that Toby was the (naughtier, naughtiest) puppy she had ever known.
8. He played (harder, hardest) than his brother.
9. He stayed awake (later, latest) than his sister.
10. He kept Jean (busier, busiest) than the mother dog.
11. He was the (happier, happiest) puppy in the litter.
12. But he'll never be the (bigger, biggest) dog.

B. Add -er or -est to the end of each adjective to complete the sentences.

1. Tim's hair is light_____ than Jamie's.
2. Who has the dark_____ hair in class?
3. Ida has straight_____ hair than Tina.
4. Tina has the wild_____ hairdo of all.
5. Is her hair long_____ than Jamie's?
6. February is the short_____ month of the year.
7. January is long_____ than June.
8. July is warm_____ than February.
9. March is cold_____ than July.
10. Which do you think is the cold_____ month of all?

> ■ An **adverb** is a word that describes a verb. Adverbs tell
> **how, when,** or **where.** Many adverbs end in -ly.
> EXAMPLES: He ran **quickly.** She was sad **today.**
> Water dripped **here yesterday.**

A. Circle the two adverbs in each sentence.

1. Mario smiled widely and cheerfully sang for us.
2. The children sat there quietly and listened to him.
3. Yesterday Mario practiced his song carefully.
4. Soon all the boys and girls danced happily.

B. Circle the adverb in each sentence. Then write how, when, or where to show what the adverb tells about the word it describes.

_____ 1. Jim walked quietly.

_____ 2. He sang softly as he walked.

_____ 3. Later, he ate lunch.

_____ 4. He sat there to eat.

C. Use adverbs from the list below to complete the sentences.

anxiously	quickly	Suddenly
brightly	quietly	there
hopelessly	slowly	totally

1. Sam ran _____ to the door.

2. He stood _____ for a minute.

3. _____, Sam ran out the door.

4. The sun shone _____.

5. He looked _____ over his shoulder.

6. He began to walk _____.

7. His quiet day was _____ ruined.

8. He tried _____ to make it to the party on time.

9. Finally, he knocked _____, then joined the party.

Adverbs That Compare

39

> - **Adverbs,** like adjectives, can be used to compare two or more things.
> - Most adverbs that compare two things end in -er.
>   EXAMPLE: I arrived **sooner** than you did.
> - Most adverbs that compare more than two things end in -est.
>   EXAMPLE: Ted runs the **fastest** of all the team members.
> - Sometimes more is used with a longer adverb when comparing two things. Sometimes most is used with a longer adverb when comparing more than two things.
>   EXAMPLES: I drove **more carefully** than John. Tim drove **most carefully** of all.

A. Circle the correct adverb in each sentence.

1. Jean worked (faster, fastest) than Debbie.

2. Debbie finished (later, latest) than Jean.

3. Of all the girls, Donna worked the (later, latest).

4. She wanted to be done (sooner, soonest) than Jean.

5. Debbie worked (more carefully, most carefully) of all.

6. No one tried (harder, hardest) than Debbie.

B. Complete each sentence by writing the correct form of each adverb in parentheses.

1. The swans arrived (late) _____ than the ducks.

2. Of all the birds, they flew the (quietly) _____.

3. The duck quacked (loudly) _____ than the swan.

4. The swan swam (peacefully) _____ than the duck.

5. The beautiful black swan swam the (near) _____ to me of all the birds.

6. He swam (slowly) _____ than the white swan.

7. I will be back here (soon) _____ than you.

8. The picture of the swans will be taken (carefully) _____ than my other picture.

> ■ Good is an adjective that describes nouns. Well is an adverb that tells how something is done.
> EXAMPLE: That is a **good** TV that works **well**.

A. Use good or well to complete each sentence.

1. George sings _____, and Jill is a _____ dancer.

2. They work _____ together.

3. Both George and Jill had _____ teachers.

4. They learned _____ from their teachers.

5. They perform their act _____.

6. Their piano music is very _____, too.

7. They both play the piano very _____.

8. Such _____ performers are hard to find.

9. Everyone who sees them perform has a _____ time.

10. I'm going to practice so that I can sing as _____ as George.

11. Don't you think that's a _____ idea?

> ■ Do not use a no word with another no word or after a contraction that ends with -n't. Some no words are no, none, nobody, nothing, nowhere, never, and not.
> EXAMPLES: Incorrect—**Nobody never** writes me letters.
> Correct—**Nobody ever** writes me letters.

B. Circle the correct word to complete each sentence.

1. The little boy doesn't have (no, any) paper.
2. I haven't (no, any) extra paper for him to borrow.
3. The teacher has (nothing, anything) to give him, either.
4. Doesn't he (ever, never) bring extra paper?
5. Are you sure you don't have (no, any) paper?
6. Hasn't someone got (nothing, anything) to give him?
7. Why doesn't (anybody, nobody) ever plan ahead?

> ■ Those is an adjective used to describe a noun. Them is an object pronoun and is used after a verb or a word such as at, with, to, and for.
> EXAMPLES: I like **those** shoes. I'd like to buy **them**.

A. Write them or those to complete each sentence.

1. Did you see _____ boys?

2. I have not seen _____ this afternoon.

3. If I do see _____, I'll give _____ a speech.

4. Have you seen _____ models all over their room?

5. I told _____ to put _____ models away yesterday.

6. I'd better find _____ soon.

7. Otherwise, I might make _____ models disappear!

8. I am not happy with _____ boys at all!

> ■ Doesn't is singular. Use doesn't with one person, place, or thing.
> ■ Don't is plural. Use don't with more than one and with the words you and I.
> EXAMPLES: Ed **doesn't** have a ride home. We **don't** have room in the car.

B. Write doesn't or don't to complete each sentence.

1. Juan and Charles _____ want to miss the practice.

2. Charles _____ like to be late.

3. Juan thinks it _____ matter if they're late.

4. Jamie _____ seem to care if he goes to practice.

5. Juan and Charles _____ understand why he _____ want to go.

6. The coach _____ want anyone to miss a practice.

7. He says they can't win if they _____ practice.

8. I _____ doubt that for a minute.

A. Circle the common nouns in each sentence. Underline the proper nouns.

1. Mark rode his old bicycle.
2. He rode to the town of Chester.
3. Jan lives on a farm nearby.
4. He wanted to ride the horse named Bullet.

B. Write A, L, or H to tell if the underlined verb is an action, linking, or helping verb.

_____ 1. Tony is packing tonight.

_____ 2. He leaves tomorrow.

_____ 3. He is a good camper.

_____ 4. Tony had hiked for hours.

_____ 5. He carries a big pack.

_____ 6. It looks heavy.

C. Write present, past, or future to tell the tense of each verb.

_____ 1. Lorene started a new job yesterday.

_____ 2. She likes her new job.

_____ 3. She will start working alone next Monday.

_____ 4. Lorene found the job last week.

D. Underline the pronouns in the sentences.

1. Aunt Mabel gave him a book.
2. She bought the book on sale.
3. *Lassie* is her favorite book.
4. He really likes the book, too.
5. She hoped he would be pleased.
6. They like to share their books.
7. She is finishing a mystery.
8. Then he will read it.

E. Choose the correct adjective or adverb for each sentence. Then write adjective or adverb.

_____ 1. Sam ran (faster, fastest) than Carl.

_____ 2. He had (shorter, shortest) legs than Carl.

_____ 3. Carl could run (longer, longest) than Sam.

_____ 4. He ran the (harder, hardest) of anyone.

Using What You've Learned

A. Read the paragraph. Then follow the directions.

As he stands outside the old house, Marty wonders if this is a good idea. He wants to go in, but the history of the house stops him. All of the young people in Charleston know of Mr. Bremmer and this place. Marty starts to walk toward the door. He still wonders if he should.

1. List the nouns from the paragraph in the correct column.

Common	Proper
_____	_____
_____	_____
_____	
_____	
_____	

2. Rewrite the paragraph in the past tense.

_____

_____

_____

_____

_____

B. Circle the correct verb. Rewrite the sentences.

1. Some jobs (is, are) not worth the money.

_____

2. We (agree, agrees) with that.

_____

3. Whoever (watch, watches) this place must be brave.

_____

4. Marty (is, are) not sure that he (is, are) brave enough.

_____

C. Rewrite the paragraph. Replace the underlined nouns with pronouns.

Marty got up Marty's nerve and walked to the house.
The front of the house was dark. There were faces carved
in the stone. The faces looked mean. "The faces are
strange," Marty thought. The faces scared Marty. "Oh well,
here I go," Marty said to himself.

_____

_____

_____

_____

_____

D. Choose one adjective and one adverb to complete each sentence.

Adjectives		Adverbs	
noisy	scariest	barely	slowly
brighter	shaky	ever	strangely
rusty		quieter	

1. The _____ doorknob turned _____.

2. This was the _____ job he had _____ taken.

3. Except for the _____ doorknob, it was _____
   than a library.

4. His _____ hand _____ touched the cobweb
   when he saw something awful.

5. Eyes _____ than fire were staring _____
   from the corner.

E. Circle the correct words to complete the paragraph.

"This (don't, doesn't) look good," Marty
mumbled to himself. (Them, Those) eyes belong to
something. I (don't, doesn't) (never, ever) remember
seeing (nothing, anything) like those eyes before. If I
get out of here, I'll learn my lesson (good, well). You
won't (ever, never) find me in a place like this again."

- **Capitalize** the names of people and pets.
  EXAMPLES: Laura Ingalls Wilder wrote many stories.
  Did she have a lamb named Cotton?
- Capitalize family names.
  EXAMPLES: Uncle Bob married Aunt Margie.
  Mom and Dad got married in California.

- **Rewrite these sentences using capital letters where needed.**

1. uncle george got up early today.

_____

2. He and aunt beth had a special job to do.

_____

3. uncle george and aunt beth were going to the animal shelter.

_____

4. They wanted to find a puppy for susan and michael.

_____

5. uncle george and aunt beth thought a small dog would be nice.

_____

6. But susan and michael wanted a big dog.

_____

7. uncle george saw a cute kitten named mittens.

_____

8. In the very last cage, they saw sasha.

_____

9. uncle george and aunt beth loved her at once.

_____

10. When sasha ran circles around michael, he loved her, too.

_____

Capitalizing Names of Places and Things

43

- Capitalize each word in a place name.
  EXAMPLES: Chicago, Germany, Utah, Howard School, Main Library, Missouri River
- Capitalize days of the week, months of the year, holidays, and names of monuments.
  EXAMPLES: Tuesday, February, Valentine's Day, the Lincoln Memorial

A. Rewrite these sentences using capital letters where needed.

1. Our class will spend memorial day in washington.

2. We hope to see the white house and the washington monument.

3. We also want to see the smithsonian institution.

4. The potomac river forms a border between washington and virginia.

5. The lincoln memorial is amazing to see at night.

6. The vietnam memorial gets many visitors.

7. There are many amazing sights in washington.

B. Answer these questions. Use capital letters where needed.

1. When were you born?

2. What is your address? Include the city and state.

3. What is your favorite holiday?

Capitalizing Titles

- Capitalize the first, last, and all important words in a book title. Words such as <u>a</u>, <u>an</u>, <u>and</u>, <u>but</u>, <u>by</u>, <u>for</u>, <u>in</u>, <u>of</u>, <u>on</u>, <u>from</u>, <u>the</u>, and <u>to</u> are not considered important words. They are not capitalized unless one of them is the first word in the title. Underline all titles of books.
    EXAMPLE: <u>A Present from Rosita</u>
- Capitalize titles of respect.
    EXAMPLES: Major Thomas, Doctor Freeman

A. Rewrite these names and titles correctly. Underline the book titles.

1. doctor william h. black _____

2. principal frank allen _____

3. The book: a wrinkle in time _____

4. captain william faircroft _____

5. The president of the united states _____

6. doctor laurie c. bell _____

7. The book: attack of the monster plants _____

8. major carol gates _____

9. The book: owls in the family _____

10. The book: my side of the mountain _____

B. Circle each letter that should be capitalized. Write the capital letter above it. Underline the book titles.

1. The results of principal thomas's plan are interesting.

2. He wrote to judge george king and asked for his help in finding people to speak at our school.

3. judge king got judge claire booth to speak about her book, life in the courts.

4. So ms. dias told us to read life in the courts before judge booth spoke.

5. Another suggested book is a judge's story by raymond field.

Capitalizing Abbreviations

> - Capitalize **abbreviations** of days and months.
>   EXAMPLES: Sun., Mon., Tues., Wed., Thurs., Fri., Sat.
>   November—Nov., August—Aug.
> - Capitalize abbreviations for titles of respect.
>   EXAMPLES: Mr., Mrs., Dr.
> - Capitalize an **initial,** the first letter of a name.
>   EXAMPLE: T. J. Woodhouse

A. Write the correct abbreviation for the days and months of the year.

1. Tuesday _____

2. Wednesday _____

3. Thursday _____

4. Friday _____

5. Saturday _____

6. Sunday _____

7. January _____

8. November _____

9. September _____

10. August _____

11. October _____

12. December _____

B. Rewrite these sentences using capital letters where needed.

1. Students from r.c. Field School will attend a special program.

   _____

2. mr. t. Jones will speak about school safety.

   _____

3. dr. Joan Holt will discuss what to do in an emergency.

   _____

4. The principal, mrs. Howard, invited them.

   _____

5. prof. Jones wrote an interesting book with dr. j. c. Holliday.

   _____

6. They did a study at Booker t. Washington School.

   _____

7. capt. e. m. Banks from the police department helped with the book.

   _____

- Capitalize the street name, city, and date in a letter. Also capitalize all letters in abbreviations for states. Together these words make up the **heading.**

    EXAMPLE: 1100 N. Main St.
    Hartford, CT 06105
    May 24, 1989

- Capitalize the **greeting.**

    EXAMPLE: Dear Mr. Jones,

- Capitalize the first word of the **closing.**

    EXAMPLES: Sincerely yours, Your friend,

- **Underline the letters that should be capitalized in the letters.**

7216 melvin street
houston, tx 77040
october 23, 1989

dear fred,

Our class is doing a report on farm life. Do you have any information you can send me? My report must be turned in three weeks from today. I can really use any help you can give me. Pictures and facts would be helpful. The names of some books I could find at the library would also help a lot.

your friend,
jesse

820 w. state st.
lockhart, al 36455
october 29, 1989

dear jesse,

I'll be glad to help with your report. Better yet, why don't you come and visit? Call and let me know if you are coming. The library here serves all of alabama. I know we could find all the information you need.

your best friend,
fred

> ■ Begin all sentences with a capital letter.
>   EXAMPLE: Mary rode a bike.
> ■ End a statement or a command with a **period.** (.)
>   EXAMPLE: Jake rode a bike.
> ■ End a question with a **question mark.** (?)
>   EXAMPLE: Did Jake ride a bike?
> ■ End an exclamation with an **exclamation point.** (!)
>   EXAMPLE: Ouch, I fell!

A. Begin and end each sentence correctly. Put the correct punctuation mark at the end of each sentence, and circle any letters that should be capitalized.

1. i am going to ride my bike to the store
2. where is my bike
3. it is always in the garage by the hose
4. could it be on the back porch
5. i'll ask Mother if she has seen it
6. she said it was in the garage this morning
7. oh, no, someone has stolen my bike
8. what should I do now
9. who could have taken it

B. Rewrite each sentence correctly.

1. i'll call the police about my bike

_____

2. hurry, hurry, answer the phone

_____

3. hello, is this the police station

_____

4. yes, what can we do for you

_____

5. you must help me catch a bike thief

_____

6. how do you know your bike wasn't borrowed

_____

Using Commas in Sentences

> ■ Use a **comma** (,) to take the place of the word <u>and</u> when three or more things are listed together in a sentence.
>   EXAMPLE: Mary, Pete, and George went to the beach.
> ■ Use a comma to separate the parts of a compound sentence.
>   EXAMPLE: Mary rode her bike, but Pete walked.
> ■ Use a comma to set off words such as <u>yes</u>, <u>no</u>, and <u>well</u> at the beginning of a sentence.
>   EXAMPLE: Yes, I want to ride my bike.

■ **Rewrite these sentences using commas correctly. Leave out the word <u>and</u> when possible.**

1. I called Mel and Janet and Karen last Saturday.

_____

2. Yes they wanted to have a picnic.

_____

3. Mel packed a lunch and Karen brought a backpack.

_____

4. Well we were finally ready to go.

_____

5. Yes we found a perfect place by the beach.

_____

6. We played baseball and swam and hiked.

_____

7. It was a great picnic and there were no ants around.

_____

8. We collected shells and driftwood and pebbles.

_____

9. Mel cleaned up the garbage and Karen packed the leftovers.

_____

10. On the ride home we sang and laughed and read.

_____

> ■ Use a comma to set off the name of a person spoken to.
>   EXAMPLE: Mother, you said we could go.
> ■ Use commas to set off a phrase that helps explain the subject of a sentence.
>   EXAMPLE: Mr. Gonzales, Rudy's father, is a lawyer.

A. Add commas where needed in each sentence.

1. Our neighbor Buddy Rush is gone.

2. Mr. Rush his father said he doesn't know where Buddy is.

3. Danny did Buddy talk about going somewhere?

4. This seems very strange to me Tim.

5. Chief Carter our sheriff thinks so, too.

6. Buddy where are you?

7. Danny don't you remember what I told you?

8. What should we do now Chief Carter?

B. Put an X in front of the sentence that tells about each numbered sentence.

1. René, your brother is here.

_____ René is your brother.

_____ Someone is talking to René.

2. Lydia, my friend will go, too.

_____ Lydia is my friend.

_____ Someone is talking to Lydia.

3. Our neighbor, Mrs. Hicks, is sick.

_____ Mrs. Hicks is our neighbor.

_____ Someone is talking to your neighbor.

4. Aunt Carrie, your sister is home.

_____ Aunt Carrie is your sister.

_____ Someone is talking to Aunt Carrie.

5. Anna, my dog, is loose.

_____ Anna is my dog.

_____ Someone is talking to Anna.

> - Use a comma between the city and state in the heading. Use a comma between the day and year.
>   EXAMPLE: 872 Park Street
>   Chicago, IL 60641
>   September 17, 1989
> - Use a comma following the name in the greeting.
>   EXAMPLES: Dear Nancy, Dear Uncle Bill,
> - Use a comma following the last word of the closing.
>   EXAMPLES: Sincerely yours, Your friend,

A. Add commas where needed in the letters.

422 W. South St.

Dallas TX 72843

November 12 1989

Dear Mark

Thank you for coming to my party. It was fun having you there. I also want to thank you for the great sweatshirt. It fits fine, and I really like it.

Your friend

Theresa

___

8200 Columbus Ave.

Dallas TX 72844

November 16 1989

Dear Theresa

Don't forget about the trip to the zoo on Saturday. See you there.

Sincerely

Mark

B. Add commas where they are needed in the headings.

1. 321 Pebble Beach Drive
   Jacksonville FL 32211
   November 17 1951

2. 101 Main St.
   Oakland CA 10032
   July 10 1989

C. Add commas where they are needed in the greetings and closings.

1. Dear Juana
2. Sincerely yours
3. Your best friend

4. Dear Grandmother
5. Your grandson
6. Hi, Scott

■ A **quote** tells the exact words someone says. Put **quotation marks** (" ") before and after the words. Use a comma, a period, a question mark, or an exclamation point between the quoted words and the rest of the sentence. Begin the first word of a direct quote with a capital letter.

EXAMPLES: "Why don't you eat your cereal?" asked Jack. Jenny said, "I'm not hungry."

■ **Look at the pictures. See who is talking and what is being said. Tell what each speaker said. Include the word <u>said</u> or <u>asked</u> and the name of the speaker. Add quotation marks and commas where needed.**

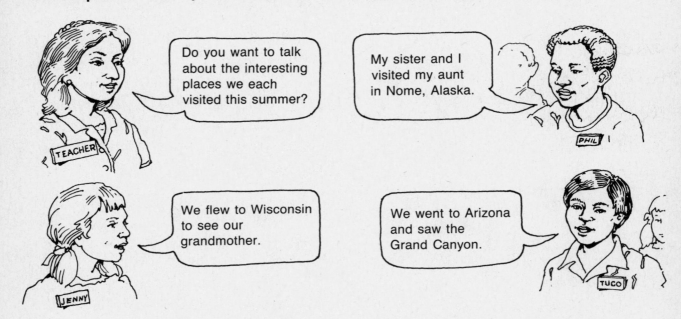

1. What did the teacher say?

   "Do you want to talk about the interesting places we each visited this summer?" asked the teacher.

2. What did Phil say?

   _____

3. What did Jenny say?

   _____

4. What did Tuco say?

   _____

More About Quotation Marks

> ■ Sometimes the speaker of a quote is named in the middle of the words being spoken. When this happens, quotation marks should be placed before and after both groups of words. Commas are placed inside the quotation marks at the end of the first group of words and again after the speaker's name.
>
> EXAMPLE: "I'd like to go," said Mary, "but I can't."

■ **Place quotation marks around the quotes. Add question marks and commas where needed.**

1. Well said Mike Dot is just getting over a strange accident.

2. What happened asked Susan.

3. A thought struck her said Mike.

4. Jake asked Why did you throw the alarm clock out the window

5. Because said Joan I wanted to see time fly.

6. What did one wall say to another asked Bonnie.

7. I'll meet you at the corner answered David.

8. What gets wetter Carlos asked the more you dry

9. A towel does said Angie.

10. Mother said Are your feet dirty

11. Yes replied Bobby but don't worry because I have my shoes on.

12. Maria asked How can you tell when an ice cube is nervous

13. It breaks out said Bill in a cold sweat.

14. Anna asked What is black-and-white and red all over

15. It's a blushing zebra said Jake.

16. What did the rug say to the floor asked Mike.

17. Don't move replied Bonnie because I've got you covered.

18. Joan asked Why do sponges do a good job

19. They become absorbed in their work said Carlos.

20. Angie asked Why is a pencil like a riddle

21. Because said Maria it's no good without a point.

> - Use an **apostrophe** (') in a contraction to show where a letter or letters are taken out.
> - Won't is an exception. will not = won't
> - Contractions can be made by joining a verb and <u>not</u>.
>   EXAMPLES: can not = can't, did not = didn't
> - Contractions can also be made by joining a noun or pronoun and a verb.
>   EXAMPLES: **It's** (it + is) a beautiful day.
>   **Susan's** (Susan + is) going to play.
>   **She'll** (she + will) have a lot of fun.

A. Circle the correct meaning for the contraction in each sentence.

1. Mother said she'll go to the store today.   (she will, she had)
2. We're supposed to clean the house.   (We will, We are)
3. My sisters say they'll clean the living room.   (they will, they would)
4. I'll clean the kitchen.   (I would, I will)
5. She's going to be home soon.   (She is, She will)
6. We'd better get moving!   (We will, We had)

B. Write the contraction for the underlined words.

1. <u>It is</u> funny that <u>we are</u> lost.

   _____   _____

2. <u>You are</u> sure <u>we have</u> followed the directions correctly?

   _____   _____

3. <u>I am</u> sure <u>they will</u> start looking for us soon.

   _____   _____

4. We <u>did not</u> bring a map, but we <u>should have</u>.

   _____   _____

5. <u>I will</u> bet that <u>we will</u> be here all night.

   _____   _____

6. <u>We are</u> in trouble now because <u>I am</u> tired.

   _____   _____

Using Apostrophes to Show Possession

> ■ Remember that apostrophes are not only used in contractions. They are also used to show ownership, or possession.
> EXAMPLES: Contraction—My **sister's** coming here.
> Possessive—My **sister's** friend is coming here. Both my **sisters'** friends are coming.

A. Rewrite each word in parentheses to show ownership. Use -'s or -s'.

1. Our family went on a picnic in my (brother) _____ car.

2. The (car) _____ windows would not roll down.

3. (Dad) _____ clothes were soaked with sweat.

4. Both my (sisters) _____ jeans were wrinkled.

5. Finally my (family) _____ terrible trip was over.

6. We arrived at our (friends) _____ house for our picnic.

B. Rewrite each sentence. Replace each underlined phrase with a phrase that includes a possessive with an apostrophe.

1. We all liked the story Jennifer told the best.

_____

2. The setting of the story was an old castle.

_____

3. There was a prison in the basement of the castle.

_____

4. The attention of the students was on Jennifer as she read.

_____

5. A cruel man lived in the tower of the castle.

_____

6. The children of the cruel man weren't allowed to play.

_____

A. Circle the letters that need to be capitalized.

1. marjorie took her horse, blaze, out for a ride.
2. she rode through placeville to the miller house.
3. mr. miller's father, judge miller, served on the indiana supreme court.
4. judge miller served from sept. 1950 to aug. 1980.
5. his record was well-known in washington.
6. senator higgins often went to him for advice.
7. marjorie and her friends loved to hear judge miller talk about his experiences.

B. Put a period, a question mark, or an exclamation point on the blank following each sentence. Add commas where needed.

5780 W. Natchez

Miles VT 05857

December 10 1989

Dear Pam

It's been a long time since my last letter___ How are you___ Everything is fine here but I really miss having you as a neighbor___ Amy our new neighbor is nice___ She goes to Taft School and she is in my class___ No she will never replace you as my best friend___ Oh I almost forgot___ Mrs. Tandy said "Tell Pam hello for me___" We all miss you a lot___ Do you still think you can visit this summer___

Your best friend

Delia

C. Add quotation marks, commas, and other punctuation marks where needed.

1. Henry stand by the door for a minute said Father.
2. What for asked Henry.
3. I want you to hold the door answered Father while I bring in this table.
4. Wow exclaimed Henry are you going to carry that by yourself?
5. It's not very heavy said Father.
6. What are you going to do with it asked Henry.
7. We need it for the kitchen said Father.

Using What You've Learned

A. Circle letters that should be capitalized. Add needed commas, periods, exclamation points, quotation marks, and apostrophes.

miriam stone WBZIs top reporter woke up early. she said
I have plenty of time to get ready. she thought of the
letter she received yesterday:

920 s. lake st
kansas city mo 43210
april 1 1988

dear miriam

   if you want a really exciting story, meet me at the j m
banister library at 10:00 o'clock tomorrow morning. Im sure
your stations news room will want this story.

yours truly
A Fan

she asked herself what it could be. miriam dressed ate
breakfast got her notebook and headed for the library. it was
not far and soon she was there.

suddenly a short woman in a dark dress walked up and
said I wrote the letter. she said you must hear my story.

my name is juanita she said. Ive been tricked by a gang
of crooks. i need your help.

miriam said tell me your story and I'll see what I can do

juanita told miriam of a man named general j c cook who
said he worked for the united states army. he told her he
needed a key to all the safety boxes in the bank where she
worked. yes she said it was strange but he said it was for
the country. now all of the boxes had been robbed and she
was sure it was general cooks work.

miriam was excited about the story. now said miriam tell
me everything you can remember about general j c cook.

wow what a story miriam said excitedly

Unit 4, Capitalization and Punctuation

65

B. Rewrite the letter. Add capital letters, periods, question marks, exclamation points, commas, quotation marks, and apostrophes where needed.

420 station st
park ridge il 60010
april 3 1989

dear aunt marge

thank you for the invitation to spend the summer with you___ mother said I think that is a great idea___ mothers going to be working hard on a special job this summer___ she was afraid that I would be spending too much time by myself___ yes your invitation has solved that problem___

what kind of clothes should I bring___ what do you think the weather will be like___ will we get to go downtown shopping___ I can hardly wait___

your niece
penny

_____

_____

_____

_____

_____

_____

_____

_____

_____

_____

_____

_____

_____

_____

Writing Sentences

> - Remember that a **sentence** is a group of words that tells a complete thought.
> - A sentence must have at least two parts—a subject and a predicate.
>
> $\quad\quad\quad\quad\quad\quad\quad$ S $\quad\quad\quad$ P
> EXAMPLE: <u>Nora Vargas</u> <u>was bored.</u>

- **Read each group of words. Then answer the questions.**

1. Nora needed a hobby.

   a. Is there a subject? _____   If so, what is it? _____

   b. Is there a predicate? _____   If so, what is it? _____

   c. Is there a complete thought? _____   Is this a sentence? _____

2. Nora finally.

   a. Is there a subject? _____   If so, what is it? _____

   b. Is there a predicate? _____   If so, what is it? _____

   c. Is there a complete thought? _____   Is this a sentence? _____

3. Will do a family history.

   a. Is there a subject? _____   If so, what is it? _____

   b. Is there a predicate? _____   If so, what is it? _____

   c. Is there a complete thought? _____   Is this a sentence? _____

4. Nora began planning.

   a. Is there a subject? _____   If so, what is it? _____

   b. Is there a predicate? _____   If so, what is it? _____

   c. Is there a complete thought? _____   Is this a sentence? _____

5. Asked questions.

   a. Is there a subject? _____   If so, what is it? _____

   b. Is there a predicate? _____   If so, what is it? _____

   c. Is there a complete thought? _____   Is this a sentence? _____

> - A **paragraph** is a group of sentences about one main idea. There are usually several sentences in a paragraph. But sometimes a paragraph is only one sentence long. The first line of a paragraph is indented.
> - A **topic sentence** is a sentence that tells the main idea of a paragraph. The topic sentence is usually the first sentence in a paragraph.

A. Read the paragraph. Underline the topic sentence.

Nora decided that she needed a hobby. She thought about different things to pick for a hobby. She thought about collecting tapes or records. Nora finally chose to do a family history as her hobby.

B. Rewrite the sentences below in paragraph form. Put the topic sentence first and underline it. Remember to indent the first sentence.

1. To get the information she needed, Nora would have to ask a lot of questions.
2. She thought about the kinds of questions she would ask.
3. She wanted to make sure that she didn't forget any questions.
4. So Nora wrote down a list of questions that she would ask each person.
5. Next, she made copies of the list.
6. She put one person's name at the top of each copy.
7. Then she was ready to talk to people.

_____

_____

_____

_____

_____

_____

_____

_____

Writing Supporting Details

> ■ Sentences with **supporting details** give more information about the main idea of a paragraph. Each sentence should contain details that support the topic sentence.

■ **Three sentences do not support the topic sentence. Draw a line through them. Then write the topic sentence and the five supporting sentences in paragraph form. Remember to indent the first sentence.**

Topic Sentence: Nora was ready to begin her history.

1. First, she put her questions into a notebook.

2. She made sure she had pens and extra paper.

3. Then Nora called Grandma and Grandpa Casey and asked when she could come and talk to them.

4. She told Grandma Casey about her new bike.

5. Grandma and Grandpa Casey are fun.

6. She also called Grandpa Vargas.

7. All of her grandparents were glad to help with the family history.

8. Many of Nora's friends had hobbies.

_____

_____

_____

_____

_____

_____

_____

_____

_____

_____

_____

58

> ■ **Time order** is used to tell things in the order in which they happened. Some words that help show time order are <u>first</u>, <u>next</u>, <u>then</u>, <u>afterward</u>, and <u>finally</u>.

■ **Number the sentences below in the order in which the events happened. Place the topic sentence first. Then write the sentences in paragraph form. Remember to indent the first sentence.**

_____ **1.** He took a train from Canada to Boston.

_____ **2.** He worked in Chicago for three years.

_____ **3.** Grandpa Casey came a long way on his journey to Sacramento.

_____ **4.** First, he traveled by coach to Dublin, Ireland.

_____ **5.** Finally, he left Chicago and drove to Sacramento.

_____ **6.** After working for five years in Boston, he took a bus to Chicago.

_____ **7.** Then he took a ship from Ireland to Canada.

_____ **8.** He lived in Canada for two years.

_____ **9.** He stayed in Dublin for only two months.

_____ **10.** Now he enjoys telling about the cities he has lived in.

_____

_____

_____

_____

_____

_____

_____

_____

_____

_____

_____

Writing a Conversation

> - When writing a **conversation,** be sure to:
>   - Use quotation marks around each quote.
>   - Use words such as <u>said</u> and <u>asked</u> with each quote.
>   - Begin a new paragraph for each quote.
>
>   EXAMPLES: Nora asked, "Will you tell me about your childhood?"
>
>   Grandpa said, "Of course I will."

- **Rewrite the paragraph as a conversation between Nora and Grandpa Vargas. Be sure to start a new paragraph for each quote.**

Nora asked Grandpa Vargas what it was like when he was growing up. Grandpa Vargas said he would tell her about his boyhood in Mexico. He said that his father raised sheep. He said that he used to watch the flock of sheep for his father. Grandpa said it was not an easy job because wolves were always nearby. Nora asked Grandpa Vargas to tell her about the wolves.

Nora asked, "What was it like when you were growing up?"

_____

_____

_____

_____

_____

_____

_____

_____

_____

_____

_____

_____

- The **topic** is the subject you are writing about. The topic of a paragraph or story should be something that interests you.
- The **audience** is the person or people who will read what you wrote. Before starting to write, ask yourself some questions: Who will read this? How old are the people who will read this? What kinds of things are they interested in?

A. Next to the list of topics, write <u>adult</u>, <u>teenager</u>, or <u>child</u> to show who might be most interested in the topic.

_____ 1. A story about the amount of gas different car models use

_____ 2. A picture book about baby animals

_____ 3. A story about dirt-bike racing

_____ 4. A travel story about Spain

_____ 5. Nursery rhymes

_____ 6. A story about a rock group's travels

_____ 7. A story about teenage movie stars

_____ 8. Fairy tales

_____ 9. The life story of a famous writer

_____ 10. A book of riddles

_____ 11. A book about home remodeling

B. Write five topics that are interesting. Then write the audience that you think might be interested in each topic.

Topic	Audience
1. _____	_____
2. _____	_____
3. _____	_____
4. _____	_____
5. _____	_____

Planning an Outline

- An **outline** is a plan to help organize writing. An outline lists the main ideas of a topic.
- An outline starts with a **statement** that tells the topic of the writing. The statement is followed by **main headings** and **subheadings** that tell what goes into each part. Main headings start with a roman numeral. Subheadings start with a capital letter.

Statement: Grandpa Vargas's life

(Main Heading)   I. Childhood

(Subheadings) {   A. Born in Mexico
                B. Moved to the U.S.

           II. Adult Years
                A. Worked in factory
                B. Started grocery store

- **Choose one of your topics from page 72. Write an outline for that topic. Use the sample outline as a guide.**

Statement: _____

    I. _____

       A. _____

       B. _____

   II. _____

       A. _____

       B. _____

  III. _____

       A. _____

       B. _____

  IV. _____

       A. _____

       B. _____

> ■ A **narrative paragraph** tells a story. A narrative paragraph usually tells events in the order in which they happened.

■ **Read the model paragraph. Then follow the directions.**

"Ah," said Grandpa, "my meeting with the wolf was very exciting. We had just arrived at the meadow. This day, the sheep would not settle down. Blanco, my dog, was acting strangely, too. He kept circling the sheep, trying to keep them in a tight group. Suddenly, Blanco leaped on the back of one sheep and raced across the flock, back by back. Then, from a bunch of bushes, raced a huge gray form. 'Wolf!' my mind screamed, 'Wolf!' Blanco reached the edge of the flock just as the wolf did. Without slowing down, Blanco threw himself at the wolf. Next, I grabbed a stick and ran toward the wolf. I yelled and yelled and swung with the stick. I don't think I really ever touched the wolf. I was too scared to aim. Finally, I think he just got tired of all the noise we were making. He turned and trotted away. He didn't run, though. He made sure we knew that he wasn't afraid of us. Afterward, Blanco and I were very proud of ourselves."

1. Underline the topic sentence, and circle the time order words.
2. List the events of the story in the proper time order and in your own words.

    1. They had just arrived at the meadow.

_____

_____

_____

_____

_____

_____

_____

_____

_____

To write a narrative paragraph, follow these steps:
- Choose a topic, or subject.
- Decide who your audience will be.
- Write a topic sentence.
- Add supporting details.
- Use time order words to help the reader know when the events happened.

■ **Choose a topic for a narrative paragraph. Write a topic sentence that will be the first sentence of your paragraph. Then add supporting sentences to complete the paragraph.**

Topic: _____

Topic Sentence: _____

_____

Paragraph:

_____

_____

_____

_____

_____

_____

_____

_____

_____

_____

_____

_____

_____

_____

A. Write sentence if the group of words is a sentence. If the group of words is not a sentence, add whatever is needed to make it a sentence. Then write the completed sentence on the line.

1. Nora loved her grandparents' stories.

_____

2. Could listen for hours.

_____

3. Her grandparents' lives had been so exciting!

_____

B. Rewrite the sentences below in paragraph form. Put the topic sentence first and underline it. Circle the time order words.

1. Next, they'd give their names to the person playing the guessing game.
2. Finally, they'd reappear, and the person would have to guess which twin was Sean and which twin was Patrick.
3. Grandpa's twin brothers had fun playing guessing games.
4. Then the twins would hide.
5. First, Sean and Patrick would dress in clothes that looked alike.

_____

_____

_____

_____

_____

_____

_____

_____

_____

_____

A. Choose a topic about an event.

Topic: _____

B. Try to limit your topic to one statement that explains it.

Statement: _____

_____

C. Write a short outline about your topic listing the major points you want to include. You might want to include the time, the place, the people involved, the actual event, any comments made about the event, and your feelings about the event.

   I. _____

      A. _____

      B. _____

  II. _____

      A. _____

      B. _____

 III. _____

      A. _____

      B. _____

      C. _____

 IV. _____

      A. _____

      B. _____

  V. _____

      A. _____

      B. _____

      C. _____

D. Write a topic sentence about your topic.

Topic Sentence: _____

_____

E. Write a narrative paragraph. Begin with your topic sentence. Refer to your outline for supporting sentences. Remember to indent the first sentence.

_____

_____

_____

_____

_____

_____

_____

_____

_____

_____

_____

_____

_____

_____

_____

_____

_____

_____

_____

- **Alphabetical order** is often used to organize names or words on a list. Use the first letter of each word to put the words in the order of the alphabet.
- If two words begin with the same letter, look at the second letter to see which would come first.   EXAMPLE: **f**a**n**, **f**i**ne**
- If the first and second letters are the same, look at the third letter.   EXAMPLE: fi**ne**, fi**re**

- **Read the groups of topics you have studied in this book. Number the terms in each group in alphabetical order.**

1. homonyms _____

   synonyms _____

   antonyms _____

   suffixes _____

   prefixes _____

   contractions _____

   vocabulary _____

   opposites _____

2. index _____

   accent _____

   pronunciation _____

   definitions _____

   alphabetical _____

   dictionaries _____

   respellings _____

   titles _____

   copyright _____

3. statements _____

   sentences _____

   commands _____

   subjects _____

   predicates _____

   exclamations _____

   questions _____

   run-ons _____

4. capitalization _____

   punctuation _____

   abbreviations _____

   initials _____

   quotes _____

   commas _____

   closing _____

   greeting _____

   periods _____

5. adjectives _____

   nouns _____

   verbs _____

   adverbs _____

   pronouns _____

   apostrophes _____

   possessives _____

   tenses _____

6. topics _____

   paragraphs _____

   details _____

   conversations _____

   sentences _____

   titles _____

   narrative _____

   audience _____

   outlines _____

> ■ **Guide words** are at the top of each page in a dictionary. Guide words tell the first and last words listed on each page. Every word listed on the page comes between the guide words.
>   EXAMPLE: **million / modern:** The word <u>minute</u> will appear on the page. The word <u>music</u> will not.

A. Circle each word that would be on a page with these guide words.

1. alive / arrest	2. flame / fourth	3. settle / sink
anxious	fourth	side
amount	flower	shawl
accept	fog	seed
arrest	figure	seventeen
actor	fly	sink
alive	flame	service
also	fox	settle
adventure	flew	sign
ant	from	sleep
ashes	flight	shelter
allow	fruit	space

B. Rewrite each group of words in alphabetical order. Then write the words that would be the guide words for each group.

1. _____ / _____

lawn _____

last _____

lamp _____

late _____

lap _____

lake _____

lead _____

2. _____ / _____

palm _____

page _____

pass _____

pad _____

pack _____

pan _____

pat _____

> - Each word listed in a dictionary is followed by a respelling of the word. The respelling shows how to **pronounce,** or say, the word. The respelling is in parentheses following the entry word.
> - **Accent marks** show which word parts are said with the most force.   EXAMPLE: freedom (frē′ dəm)   duty (do͞o′ tē)
> - A **pronunciation key** (shown below) contains letters and special symbols, along with sample words, that show how the letters should be pronounced.

A. Write the word from the box for each respelling. Use the pronunciation key on the right.

gallop	hug	trout
girl	huge	vanish
glide	lowly	write

at; āpe; fär; câre; end; mē; it; īce; pîerce; hot; ōld; sông; fôrk; oil; out; up; ūse; rüle; pu̇ll; tûrn; chin; sing; shop; thin; this; hw in white; zh in treasure. The symbol ə stands for the unstressed vowel sound in about, taken, pencil, lemon, and circus.

1. (gûrl) _____

2. (lō′ lē) _____

3. (rīt) _____

4. (trout) _____

5. (glīd) _____

6. (hūj) _____

7. (gal′ əp) _____

8. (hug) _____

9. (van′ ish) _____

B. Complete each sentence. Write the word in the blank next to its respelling.

dictionary	found	guide	respelling	word

1. David didn't know how to say the (wûrd) _____ protection.

2. He took out his (dik′ shə ner′ ē) _____.

3. He used (gīd) _____ words to find the page.

4. Then he (found) _____ the word.

5. The (rē spel′ ing) _____ was listed right after the word. It wasn't so hard to say after all.

Dictionary: Definitions

> - The **definition,** or meaning, is given for each word listed in a dictionary. Some words have more than one meaning. Then each meaning is numbered.
> - The **parts of speech** are also given for each word.
>   EXAMPLE: **hard** (härd) *adj.* **1.** very firm. **2.** difficult.

A. Use the dictionary entries below to answer the questions.

barrier (bar′ ē ər) *n.* **1.** something that blocks progress or the way: *The deep river was an impossible barrier for the horseback riders to cross.* **2.** something that separates or divides: *Their age difference was a barrier.* **3.** something that hinders or limits: *His lack of good study habits was a barrier to higher grades.*
beam (bēm) *n.* **1.** a piece of long wood, iron, or steel ready to use in building. **2.** a ray of light: *The ship's beam shone through the fog.* **3.** a bright gleam or look: *The baby's smile was a beam of joy.*
bold (bōld) *adj.* **1.** having courage; fearless: *The first pilots were bold men.* **2.** impolite; rude: *The bold man cut in line.* **3.** standing out clearly: *The setting sun had bold orange colors.*
borrow (bôr′ ō) *v.* **1.** to get or take something with the understanding that it must be returned: *The library allows cardholders to borrow books for one month.* **2.** to take or use from another source and use as one's own; adopt: *Many words we use today are borrowed from foreign languages.*

n.	noun
pron.	pronoun
v.	verb
adj.	adjective
adv.	adverb
prep.	preposition

1. How many definitions are given for the word barrier? _____

   for the words beam and bold? _____   for the word borrow? _____

2. What does the abbreviation v. following the respelling of

   borrow stand for? _____

3. Which words in the dictionary sample are nouns? _____

4. What part of speech is bold? _____

B. Write the number of the dictionary definition used for the underlined word.

1. _____ A barrier kept the fans off the playing field.

2. _____ The congressman borrowed a joke from one of his aides to use in his opening speech.

3. _____ The flashlight's beam led the campers to their tent.

4. _____ Wooden beams were used to build the barn.

5. _____ The bold captain led his ship through the hurricane.

6. _____ Her Hawaiian-print shirt has bold colors.

Parts of a Book

- The **title page** tells the name of a book and the name of its author.
- The **copyright page** tells who published the book, where it was published, and when it was published.
- The **table of contents** lists the chapter or unit titles and the page numbers on which they begin. It is at the front of a book.
- The **index** gives a detailed list of the topics in a book. It gives the page numbers for each topic. It is at the back of a book.

- **Use this book to answer the questions.**

1. What is the title of this book?

   _____

2. On what page does Unit Three start? _____

3. List the pages that deal with apostrophes. _____

4. What is the copyright date of this book? _____

5. Who are the authors of this book?

   _____

6. On what page is the lesson on prefixes? _____

7. On what page does Unit Six start? _____

8. Where is the index? _____

9. List the pages that deal with adverbs. _____

10. What lesson is on page 42? _____

11. On what pages are the lessons on action verbs? _____

12. What company published this book?

    _____

13. What lesson is on page 79?

    _____

A. Write the number of the dictionary definition used for the underlined word.

messenger (mes′ ən jər) *n.* **1.** one who picks up and delivers messages and packages. **2.** a sign of things to come: *The dark clouds are a messenger of the oncoming storm.*

rake (rāk) *v.* **1.** to gather loose items or to smooth with a rake: *In the fall we must rake many leaves.* **2.** to search for carefully: *They raked the airport for their lost luggage.*

1. _____ Longer days are a <u>messenger</u> of the coming warm weather.

2. _____ The <u>messenger</u> travels around the city on a bicycle.

3. _____ The bus driver <u>raked</u> through his coat pockets but couldn't find the keys.

B. Write the words in alphabetical order under the correct guide words.

1. **dear / delicious**

_____

_____

_____

_____

2. **delight / develop**

_____

_____

_____

_____

depend
degree
debt
den
defend
demand
design
deck

C. Complete each sentence. Write the word in the blank next to its respelling.

1. If you (nēd) _____ help with a word, look in the dictionary.

2. The (dik′ shə ner′ ē) _____ tells you what a word means.

3. It also tells you how to (sā) _____ the word.

4. Often, the word is given in a (sen′ təns) _____.

dictionary
need
say
sentence

D. Write <u>title page</u>, <u>copyright page</u>, <u>table of contents</u>, or <u>index</u> to tell where to find this information.

_____ 1. The chapter titles in the book.

_____ 2. The year the book was published.

_____ 3. The title of the book.

_____ 4. The page number on which a certain topic can be found.

A. Use a social studies book to complete the exercise.

1. Find the title on the title page of the book.

   Write the title. _____

2. Find the name of the publisher and the year it was published.

   Write this information. _____

3. Find the names of the authors.

   Write the names. _____

4. How many sections or chapters are there in the book?

   Write the number. _____

5. Look carefully at the index.

   How are the words in the index listed? _____

6. Choose a person you have already studied this year in social studies.

   Write the person's name. _____

7. Look in the index for page numbers on which information about this person can be found.

   Write the page numbers. _____

8. In what chapter or chapters does the information about this person appear?

   Write the chapter numbers. _____

B. Look up the word <u>happiness</u> in a dictionary. Then follow the directions below.

1. Tell what part of speech <u>happiness</u> is. _____

2. Copy the first definition. _____

3. Write a sentence using the word <u>happiness</u>. _____

   _____

4. Copy the respelling. _____

C. Rewrite the words in alphabetical order. Then find the words in a dictionary. Next to each word, write the guide words from the top of the page and the respelling of the word.

most	pity	remind	door	ancient
blizzard	scent	magician	faucet	venture
ramp	money	ache	perfect	disease
helpful	paint	case	howl	cheerful

	Words	Guide Words	Respelling
1.	ache	accuse / acorn	āk
2.			
3.			
4.			
5.			
6.			
7.			
8.			
9.			
10.			
11.			
12.			
13.			
14.			
15.			
16.			
17.			
18.			
19.			
20.			

Synonyms and Antonyms ▪ Write <u>S</u> if the underlined words are synonyms. Write <u>A</u> if they are antonyms.

_____ 1. Miguel was <u>pleased</u> and <u>happy</u> to join the team.

_____ 2. Last year his team <u>won</u> many games but <u>lost</u> the championship.

_____ 3. Miguel felt <u>little</u> next to his <u>huge</u> teammates.

_____ 4. Miguel was <u>quiet</u> as they walked onto the <u>silent</u> field.

Homonyms ▪ Circle the correct homonym to complete each sentence.

1. Joe and Jane did not (hear, here) the alarm.
2. They were (to, too, two) tired to pay attention.
3. They were surprised to see (to, too, two) men run from the store.
4. The police asked Joe and Jane to (write, right) down what they saw.

Contractions ▪ Write the two words that make up each underlined contraction.

_____ 1. Joe <u>couldn't</u> understand how they got away.

_____ 2. They <u>didn't</u> see where either of the men went.

_____ 3. They were sorry they <u>weren't</u> paying attention.

_____ 4. "<u>We've</u> got to stop walking around in a fog," Jane told Joe.

_____ 5. "Yes, we <u>would've</u> seen where they went, had we been more alert," agreed Joe.

Prefixes, Suffixes, and Compound Words ▪ Write <u>P</u> if the underlined word has a prefix. Write <u>S</u> if it has a suffix. Write <u>C</u> if it is two words joined to make a compound word.

_____ 1. The thieves robbed a <u>drugstore</u>.

_____ 2. Both of them <u>disappeared</u>.

_____ 3. One <u>rethought</u> what he had done.

_____ 4. He knew it was <u>useless</u> to hide.

_____ 5. A <u>policewoman</u> found the other.

_____ 6. Her search had been <u>useful</u>.

_____ 7. The thief was hiding <u>upstairs</u>.

_____ 8. Both thieves felt very <u>unlucky</u>.

Recognizing Sentences ▪ Write <u>S</u> if the group of words is a sentence. Write <u>X</u> if the group of words is not a sentence.

_____ 1. Do you need?

_____ 2. Something from the store.

_____ 3. I need some milk and bread.

_____ 4. I'll get them for you.

_____ 5. If I.

_____ 6. I'll go before noon.

_____ 7. Then we can make lunch.

_____ 8. Before Betty and Jim return.

Types of Sentences ▪ Write <u>declarative</u>, <u>interrogative</u>, <u>imperative</u>, or <u>exclamatory</u> to show what type each sentence is.

_____ 1. Do you have a ticket to the game?

_____ 2. Oh, no, I left my ticket at home!

_____ 3. A new ticket costs a dollar.

_____ 4. Lend me some money.

_____ 5. I'll pay you back tomorrow.

Subjects and Predicates ▪ Draw one line under the subject and two lines under the predicate in each sentence. Then circle the simple subject and the simple predicate.

1. Our class went on a picnic.

2. The picnic was at the city zoo.

3. We saw some very strange animals.

4. Many in the class had been to the zoo before.

5. Some students liked the bears the best.

6. Everyone in the class enjoyed the dolphin show.

7. Twelve boys came to the first practice.

8. The coach wanted girls on the team, too.

9. He delayed the first practice until the next day.

10. Eight girls finally joined the team.

Nouns—Proper and Common ▪ Circle the common nouns, and underline the proper nouns.

1. Sally sat next to the window.

2. It was a wonderful morning in June.

3. Warm mornings in California are very beautiful.

Nouns—Singular, Plural, and Possessive ▪ Circle the correct form of each noun.

1. Our (dogs, dog's) puppies are brown and white.

2. All the (puppy's, puppies') ears are long.

3. Our other (dogs, dog's) stay away from the puppies.

4. The puppies' (tail's, tails) are always wagging.

Verbs ▪ Circle the correct verb to complete each sentence.

1. William (is, are) in the school play.

2. He (went, gone) to two tryouts before he was chosen.

3. The school has (give, given) a play every year.

4. The students (have, has) always taken part.

5. William (try, tried) hard to get a part in the play.

Pronouns ▪ Underline the pronoun in each sentence. Write S for subject, O for object, or P for possessive for each pronoun.

_____ 1. Marie had to fix her bike.

_____ 2. She checked all of the parts.

_____ 3. The bike was given to her.

_____ 4. Tom gave her the bike.

_____ 5. He is Marie's brother.

_____ 6. His new bike is bigger.

Adjectives and Adverbs ▪ Write adjective or adverb for each underlined word.

_____ 1. Terri walked slowly into the room.

_____ 2. Her bright jacket seemed out of place.

_____ 3. Her shaky voice showed how scared she was.

_____ 4. My kind friend put her arm around Terri.

_____ 5. Suddenly, Terri looked much more comfortable.

Capitalization and Punctuation ▪ Rewrite the letter below. Add capital letters, periods, commas, question marks, and quotation marks where needed.

---

328 n state st

new york ny 10010

january 2 1979

dear dr turner

  I want to thank you for your kindness to tootsie my pet bird my friend jack said, no one knows how to cure birds they're different from other types of pets you shouldn't waste your money can you believe that I didn't agree with jack, so I brought tootsie to your office thanks to you, tootsie is fine again

        sincerely

        juan gomez

Topic Sentences and Supporting Details ▪ **Circle the topic sentence. Underline only the supporting details.**

Martin wanted a spot on the bowling team. First, he got a colorful bowling shirt. Then he bought a new ball. He polished that ball every single day. He went home for lunch. Finally, he bought the best bowling shoes he could afford.

Time Order Words ▪ **List the time order words from the paragraph above.**

1. _____   2. _____   3. _____

Conversation ▪ **Rewrite the paragraph as a conversation between Dave and Martin. Be sure to start a new paragraph for each quote.**

Dave asked Martin if he was ready for the team tryouts. Martin said that he was. He also said he was sure that he had done everything possible to get on the team. Dave wished him luck. Then Martin groaned as he said that he knew he had forgotten something. Dave asked Martin what he could have forgotten. Martin told Dave he had forgotten his bowling ball!

_____

_____

_____

_____

_____

_____

_____

_____

_____

_____

_____

_____

_____

Alphabetical Order and Guide Words ▪ Rewrite each list in alphabetical order. Then write the words that would be the guide words for each list.

Guide Words

_____ / _____

1. right _____

2. rock _____

3. rich _____

4. rinse _____

5. rob _____

6. rib _____

7. royal _____

Guide Words

_____ / _____

1. bat _____

2. back _____

3. ball _____

4. base _____

5. baby _____

6. bank _____

7. bark _____

Pronunciation ▪ Use a dictionary to find each word listed. Write the respelling of each word.

1. now _____

2. later _____

3. tomorrow _____

4. today _____

5. direct _____

6. scissors _____

7. moccasin _____

8. responsible _____

9. coin _____

10. pasture _____

11. bargain _____

12. thumb _____

Parts of a Book ▪ Write title page, copyright page, table of contents, or index to tell where you would find this information.

_____ 1. A chapter title

_____ 2. The page on which certain information can be found

_____ 3. The author's name

_____ 4. The year the book was published